ADOPTING
a Great Dog

TS-293

About Our Cover Dog

Not Maximillian, Maxwell, or Maximum, just MAX. He's sturdy, dependable, and "the most"—and he was adopted at the tender age of three months by Marcy Myerovich and her family in Brick Township, New Jersey. Today Max is fourteen years old, and while slowing down, he is still the irrepressibly spunky all-American dog that he's ever been. Perhaps Max's greatest attribute is his love for his mom Marcy, who unashamedly spoils him with homecooking, a warm bed, nice long walks around their shoreside home, and plenty of the good life. Despite the three pairs of dress shoes puppy Max destroyed in his first month, Max grew into a true gentleman, graceful yet feisty, a reliable protector of mom and family, a good dancer (he polkas on his hinds for returning family members), and of course, the best friend any person could ask for.

Photography: Nona Kilgore Bauer, Phil Bellis, Tara Darling, Isabelle Francais, Gillian Lisle, Jean Mitchell, Alice Pantfoeder, Robert Pearcy, Vince Serbin, and Karen Taylor.

© **1997 by T.F.H. Publications, Inc.**

Distributed in the UNITED STATES to the Pet Trade by T.F.H. Publications, Inc., One T.F.H. Plaza, Neptune City, NJ 07753; distributed in the UNITED STATES to the Bookstore and Library Trade by National Book Network, Inc. 4720 Boston Way, Lanham MD 20706; in CANADA to the Pet Trade by H & L Pet Supplies Inc., 27 Kingston Crescent, Kitchener, Ontario N2B 2T6; Rolf C. Hagen Inc., 3225 Sartelon St. Laurent-Montreal Quebec H4R 1E8; in CANADA to the Book Trade by Vanwell Publishing Ltd., 1 Northrup Crescent, St. Catharines, Ontario L2M 6P5 ; in ENGLAND by T.F.H. Publications, PO Box 15, Waterlooville PO7 6BQ; in AUSTRALIA AND THE SOUTH PACIFIC by T.F.H. (Australia), Pty. Ltd., Box 149, Brookvale 2100 N.S.W., Australia; in NEW ZEALAND by Brooklands Aquarium Ltd. 5 McGiven Drive, New Plymouth, RD1 New Zealand; in Japan by T.F.H. Publications, Japan—Jiro Tsuda, 10-12-3 Ohjidai, Sakura, Chiba 285, Japan; in SOUTH AFRICA by Lopis (Pty) Ltd., P.O. Box 39127, Booysens, 2016, Johannesburg, South Africa. Published by T.F.H. Publications, Inc.
MANUFACTURED IN THE
UNITED STATES OF AMERICA
BY T.F.H. PUBLICATIONS, INC.

ADOPTING
a Great Dog

NONA
KILGORE BAUER

Acknowledgments

The author wishes to acknowledge the people who contributed their time, effort, talent and love to make this book possible.

To the Quincy, Illinois Animal Shelter and Humane Society, for working with me so patiently during very stressful times, but especially for the exceptional love and care they give to each animal who passes through their door.

To the Humane Society of Missouri, for the standard of excellence they set in the world of animal welfare.

To my editor and friend, Andrew De Prisco, for his support and encouragement and his continued faith in the challenges he offers me.

To my mentor and dear friend Dollie Wilson, who understands why I care about each nuance, period and comma and who endures each editorial process.

To my husband, for his patience and long-suffering during the writing process and his belief that I will muddle through.

Finally, to my devoted Golden Retrievers, who love and adore me even as they suffer through each book.

God bless you, one and all.

Contents

Foreword

Dogs are a phenomenon. As I interviewed the owners of shelter and rescue dogs for this book, I was struck by one common thread in their descriptions of their dogs: almost every dog was "perfect" and perfect from the very first day. No accidents, no rampant destruction, no blatant disrespect for their new human leaders. Some of the dogs had been abused and badly neglected, but still they bonded instantly to their new person. Wow! What a testimonial to the dog as man's best friend. Sure, a couple were a bit emotional, one hung out under the coffee table for a while before feeling completely safe or worried when a man approached, but overall, the dogs just walked in and made themselves at home.

There is no doubt these dogs were in fact not "perfect," but their new owners didn't see those flaws, they only saw the love. And those few who had to work to rehabilitate their dogs, especially the foster parents, said it wasn't all that bad and it was surely worth the effort! These happy stories made me feel guilty that I raise purebred dogs when there are so many needy and worthy dogs to be rehomed. I hope they touch you also, and then maybe there'll be one less dog that needs a home.

Opposite page: Raina, owned by Todd and Sandi Stephenson; Paddywack, owned by Darryl DeGreef; Peabody, owned by Jean Mitchell; Samson, owned by the Lance Hellwig family; Taffy, owned by Maxine Spangler.

"Taffy"

"Peabody"

"Raina"

"Paddywack"

"Samson"

Keeper

When Kurt and Suzanne McGee decided to get a puppy for their 12-year-old son, Kurt, they did everything right, read numerous books on dog breeds and training and caring for dogs, visited pet shops, checked ads in the local newspaper and talked to friends and veterinarians. "We considered every aspect of the responsibility, cost and inconvenience of dog ownership," Suzanne said. A visit to the animal shelter had always been part of their plan.

"There were so many wagging tails and hopeful eyes that it was difficult to walk away, but we found ourselves returning again and again to an 11-week-old yellow puppy who seemed to be taking his crate confinement in stride. He seemed ideal for us. But then the bad news came...they couldn't release the puppy for a week in case the owner came to claim him. Still he had won our hearts and we kept going to visit him, hoping each time he'd still be there.

"Finally the long week was over and we could actually touch and hold our puppy. He was so frisky and excited once he was romping about, not at all like the quiet little fellow in his crate. We were glad we had come prepared with a leash and collar and his crate. He was squirming and bouncing all over the place but he was a keeper, and that's what we decided to call him.

"Keeper started obedience class at five months old and learned to sit, stay, lie down, shake hands, jump through a hoop, fetch, and catch objects in mid-air. None of this happened overnight however. We spent time every day reinforcing the lessons and reviewing our pet owner manuals to make sure we were being consistent. It also helped us practice patience and to anticipate Keeper's response to our training. His favorite thing is a human touch and he's never met a man, woman or child he didn't like."

"Keeper"

Shelter and Rescue Dogs: Who Are They?

THE YELLOW DOG

We first saw him rummaging about in our front bushes...a long-legged yellow Lab eagerly sniffing all the tantalizing dog smells deposited by our family of five Golden Retrievers. We watched him snuffle every twig or stick that had been walked on, chewed on or anointed. Finally, satisfied with his shrubbery inspection, he trotted up to our front door and just stood there, furiously wagging his tail, waiting to be invited in.

Here obviously was a dog who was accustomed to spending time in a house. Dogs who live most of their life outside in a yard or dog pen (it shouldn't happen but it does) don't know about front or back doors nor would they expect to be allowed inside.

After an eternity of two or three minutes, the dog made no attempt to toddle off back to a master who was nowhere to be seen. The blacktop road near our farm is like many rural highways, a popular dumping ground for dogs.

Little Orphan Annie hopes that she won't be an orphan forever. She is awaiting adoption at the Quincy Humane Society.

It's not uncommon to see stray dogs traveling alone or with a canine buddy, looking for a handout or a safe place to rest. The yellow dog had found such a place. Of course we took him in.

He wore no collar and his fur showed no signs of having worn one. He was clean and in good shape, no battle scars, so he hadn't been "on the road" very long. We called him simply "Yellow Dog" and he easily settled into our family dog routine. He was a real sugarplum who loved hugging more than eating and would leave his food pan to get his ears scratched at every opportunity. What kind of person would "lose" or "dump" this sweetheart of a dog?

We spent the next two weeks searching for his owner, calling our neighbors and checking with the animal warden of our small town. No luck.

Does this story have a happy ending? The good news is that in this part of the Midwest Labradors are good candidates for adoption, and the Quincy IL Humane Society, 50 miles away, agreed to help find a home for Yellow Dog. Three weeks later he was bouncing around in a new backyard, playing with six kids who thought he was the very best dog they ever owned.

The bad news is that Yellow Dog was one of the lucky ones, one of that small percentage of stray and abandoned dogs who find a happy home. Most strays end up euthanized because there are too many "Yellow Dogs" and too few people willing to adopt them.

Sadly, only a small percentage of shelter dogs find a happy home.

Yellow Dog is also typical of many dogs who end up on a rural highway or at a shelter's doorstep. He's a "fast-food" dog, the throwaway pet that has become as common as the plastic bottles and fast-food containers that litter our beaches and parking lots. In this modern era of disposable everything, people look to rid themselves of anything inconvenient or unwanted. And shamefully, that often includes their pets, animals who have outgrown their novelty or cute stage, or just plain grew up. Too big, too rambunctious, too hairy...certainly not the dog's fault. Sadly, the most common reasons for dog abandonment are the fault of the owner, not the dog.

Abandoned Dogs: Some Reasons

Shelters and breed rescue organizations can rattle off a long list of reasons why owners give up their dogs. Many are frivolous, a few of them legitimate, but none would happen at all if people thought more about the animals before they got them in the first place. Here are some of the more common excuses owners offer when turning in their dog.

BEHAVIOR PROBLEMS

More dogs are taken to shelters for bad or inappropriate behavior than for any other reason. An estimated 7.5 million pets enter animal shelters each year, many turned in by their owners for behavior problems. A study by the Morris Animal Foundation found that behavioral problems were the leading cause of death in dogs. "He barks too much...chews too much...digs in the flower bed...runs away...jumps on the kids...guards his food dish..." the list goes on and on. In 1996 one veterinary journal reported that 50 percent of puppies who were adopted or purchased would not be in their original homes one year later. Three-quarters of those pups would be abandoned because the puppy "misbehaved." The study observed that those puppies who end up in shelters or dumped along the road have little prospect of getting a second chance in life. Back-up statistics from the American Society for the Prevention of Cruelty to Animals state that 80 percent of household pets in the United States will not die in their first home. We are a nation of disposable pet owners.

Most behavior problems are preventable. Bad behaviors occur because the owner didn't take the time to train the dog, didn't understand the dog's natural behaviors or how to communicate in canine terms. Don't let that happen to you and your new companion. Before you decide to adopt a dog, be certain you will have enough time to exercise, train and play with him. Dogs are social creatures and need to feel loved and wanted. And like children, they also need to be taught how to behave in the human world.

Candy is an Italian Greyhound who was turned in to an animal shelter as untrainable and incorrigible. She was adopted by Barbara Riley, who spent months helping her overcome her fear of everything. Candy has since mastered obedience training and earned her CD title.

When Quincy was 13 months old, his owner no longer had time for him and contacted the author to assist in placing the dog in a new home. Five minutes after meeting Quincy, there was no doubt that he would become a part of her own Golden family. He went on to earn his CD, SH, WCX, and CGC titles.

NOT ENOUGH TIME

Some owners surrender well-behaved dogs simply because the family has developed other interests and no longer has time to tend the dog, or they never had enough time to begin with and didn't realize that. In the typical family, the kids are into sports, mom gets a new job, or everyone's too busy or too tired. Too bad. The dog is always in the way. It speaks well of the dog who lives through such neglect without developing serious behavior problems. Such dogs offer great adoption potential. When adopted they are usually so grateful for love and attention from their new owner that they adjust quickly into their new environment and family structure.

DEATH OR DIVORCE

The most tragic reason for surrender is the death of the owner. Suddenly a dog who is loved and cared for is left homeless because his owner dies. Most people fail to consider what will happen to their pet in the event of their death or the death of their spouse. Sometimes the surviving spouse is unable or unwilling to care for the dog, so the dog becomes a victim along with the departed owner.

manner. Their reason: together in people-dog heaven, which makes euthanasia a comfortable choice.

Divorce spells the same heartache for the dog. It's "his" or "hers," and often the dog has to go. The dog didn't cause any problems, but he suddenly becomes one.

Dogs who are victims of death or divorce are usually well-behaved pets who will gladly offer their allegiance to a new owner, given a reasonable adjustment

Large, active dogs like this yellow Labrador need lots of room to run. The Gardner family rescued four-year-old Bogart from his second home. Now he lives the good life with two Labrador companions at the Jersey Shore.

All dog owners should include their pet(s) in the provisions of their will or state their wishes in writing as to the disposition of the dog in the event of death. Be sure a family member or a friend is willing to care for the dog or agrees to place it in a new and loving home. Some owners who have aging dogs prefer that their dogs be euthanized when the owner dies and the dog's remains buried or disposed of in a certain

period. The dog won't understand why he's suddenly "homeless" and may be cautious or suspicious of his new surroundings. Time, patience and loving care—occasionally more time than you expect, but this dog will be worth it.

WRONG CHOICE / POOR MATCH

Too many dogs are surrendered because the owners made the

wrong decision in the breed they chose. They selected a breed because it was "cute...big...small...cuddly..." without researching the character and personality of the dog or its needs. Is it easy to train, good with kids, easy to groom? That adorable puppy will grow up...and up...and up. They never knew it would be 80 pounds at nine months old! They didn't understand this was a high-energy dog who needs lots of exercise. Nor did they imagine dog hair on their white carpeting or the time involved in grooming the dog's lush fur coat.

Ike was relinquished to the animal shelter because he "needed a country life." (He barked while chained to a tree all day and night—that was his life!)

Gipper was rescued from an abusive home where he was tied to a tree all day or locked in a crate for days, sometimes without food or water. Now he is a full-time house dog and sleeps in the bed with his owners.

IMPULSE PUPPIES

Very often the puppy joined the family as an "impulse purchase." The Christmas puppy for the grandchildren, the little fluffball in the pet shop window, an irresistible puppy leftover from the litter down the street, all puppies who don't work out because of people who didn't use common dog sense to begin with.

ABUSE AND NEGLECT

Animal cruelty is against the law; in some states it's a felony. But the law still can't protect many dogs from abuse, neglect and often unspeakable cruelty at the hands of their owners. Breed rescue organizations often rescue large numbers of dogs from despicable conditions; dogs tied up and starving, dogs tortured, burned, used for fighting or as bait for fighting dogs, dogs booted out of cars speeding along the highway. Frequently many of the rescued animals are beyond help and must be destroyed. The salvageable survivors go into foster care where they are evaluated and eventually adopted. Many will require long-term rehabilitation with an adoptive family who is willing to go the extra mile in the three P's: praise, patience and persistence.

STRAYS

The majority of dogs at shelters are strays who come in through animal control or are brought in by citizens who find them wandering in backyards, scavenging in empty lots or running loose along the road. It's not uncommon for shelter personnel to arrive at work and find a box of puppies sitting at the front door or a sad and frightened dog tied to the gate. No note or explanation. No longer a problem for the owner. These dogs all arrive with question marks about the dog's temperament, health and history.

The fact is many of these discarded dogs are simply victims, good fellows who will make great pets once they are rehomed with a family who understands the needs of the individual dog and is committed to caring for the animal for his entire lifetime. The dog you adopt today can and will be as special as the dog you adored when you were growing up, as loving as the dog who shared your life for the past decade or two, even as exceptional as the dog you fantasized about owning and never could...until now.

> Tuque was adopted as a stray by **Mick and Yvonne Pertle**. He was found skinny and covered with fleas, running down the Pertles' country road foraging for food. From that first meeting, he demanded to be part of their family, bonding instantly with their two Golden Retrievers.

Scarlet was very pregnant when she was found wandering the streets. Jean Mitchell helped her to whelp her six pups in Jean's basement. The pups and Scarlet all found good homes through the humane society. This is Scarlet with one of her pups.

Snif and her adopted mom Wanda Spohr. Snif was found wandering the streets in freezing weather; she was old and starved. After a warm bath and a hot meal, Snif was given her own blue blanket to sleep on. Although she still has that bed, she chooses to sleep next to Wanda every night.

Stonewall Jackson was one of three pups left on the animal shelter doorstep at three months of age. Foster mother Jean Mitchell helped socialize him with trips to shopping malls and rides in grocery carts.

Lucy

Carole Hackett, executive director of the Quincy Humane Society adopted Lucy, a terrier mix. "Lucy came in with animal control. She had been tied to a porch for months, was half frozen and one eye was punctured. But she was still so spunky! We had her eye removed along with some tumors and I took her home. Lucy had nightmares for almost two years. I used to wonder what horrors she was dreaming about. She was very difficult to crate train but can be loose now for up to four hours. She's very mischievous and can open cabinets and bags of potato chips, which is one of her favorite foods." Carole often brings Lucy to work...that way she knows what Lucy's doing!

"Lucy"

"Barney"

Barney

Barney was orphaned at 10 years old. His master had died of cancer, and a year later his mistress passed away. The couple's daughter had three children and was unable to keep Barney, so she took him to veterinarian Joanne Klingele to be euthanized. Within 24 hours Joanne had placed Barney with Golden fanciers Andre and Janet Edmonds. He's now a happy housedog with four Golden brothers and sisters.

Shelters and Rescue Organizations

Across the United States stretches a vast network of animal shelters and rescue groups that are dedicated to saving and rehoming unwanted dogs. The people who volunteer and work for these organizations are caring and compassionate dog lovers. They have to be. Only a strong love for animals could sustain the dedication needed under such stressful conditions. Every day they care for the frightened dogs brought in by animal control and accept unwanted companions from irresponsible owners who give the dogs up for insignificant reasons. Every week they euthanize sweet little dogs because there's not enough room, time, money or willing adopters to save them all. Their greatest satisfaction is placing a dog in a permanent home with people who will love the dog forever.

That satisfaction comes too seldom, however. Shelter statistics show that nationwide, only about 25 percent of shelter dogs are rehomed, with another 15 percent reclaimed by their owners. After the waiting period required by local ordinances, the remaining 60 percent face eutha-

There are many sad "tails" of abandoned puppies in animal shelters.

A cry for help. Every week sweet little dogs are euthanized because there is not enough room, time, money or willing adopters to save them all.

nasia. Each week shelter personnel must make that life-or-death decision about each dog in their care, then carry out that gruesome task. In many cases it is the kindest act the dog will experience. Most of those unfortunate creatures at least spend their final moments with someone who cares enough to offer them a peaceful death.

ANIMAL SHELTERS

Most animal shelters operate as independent agencies. Some fall under city or county jurisdiction and operate with local tax funds. City shelters are usually staffed by local government employees. Some municipalities handle animal control through non-profit humane societies that often depend on charitable donations. Humane societies are managed by their own independent board of directors and rely heavily on volunteers and contributions.

While the operating policies of each agency vary according to state and local laws, and of course, available funds, most shelters share the common goal of finding compatible homes for as many dogs as possible. Most require spaying/neutering as a condition of adoption and offer the surgery at special rates or as part of the adoption fee.

Some animal shelters work in cooperation with the larger pet supply outlets to host "adoption days." Check local newspapers for these weekend events—or visit your nearest pet superstore.

Please "paws" to help. Most humane societies and shelters depend on volunteer help and donations.

HUMANE SOCIETIES

While government-run shelters generally function simply as temporary clearing houses for unwanted animals, humane societies often provide additional services to the pet community. Some offer pet-assisted therapy programs to area hospitals and nursing homes where volunteers take puppies, kittens and other good-natured animals on weekly visits to those institutions. Others offer discounts on obedience classes and free adoptions to senior citizens. Many shelters and humane societies work with local breed rescue volunteers when a dog of their chosen breed is unclaimed and might face euthanasia.

Neither private nor public shelters are governed by any of the well-known national humane organizations. The Humane Society of the United States (HSUS) is a nonprofit organization that promotes education to foster the humane treatment of animals. The American Humane Association (AHA) is also nonprofit and was founded in 1877 to prevent cruelty and neglect to both children and animals. The American Society for the Prevention of Cruelty to Animals (ASPCA) is the headquarters for national humane education programs and has been the official shelter for New York City since 1866.

According to the Humane Society of the United States, for every loved and cared-for dog and cat there are nine others that are homeless, in shelters or roaming the streets at the mercy of speeding cars, freezing weather and abusive human beings. An estimated 25 percent of these poor creatures are purebred dogs. Shelter statistics show that fewer than one out of every three animals that comes in will leave there alive.

Humane Society of Missouri

This is just one example of a humane society from the midwestern United States, where the author lives.

Founded in 1870, The Humane Society of Missouri is the fourth-largest and fifth-oldest humane society in the United States. The completion of their new 85,000 square foot, state-of-the-art headquarters will increase their shelter capacity by 25 percent and their veterinary medical space by 30 percent, making it the largest humane society in the country. As a not-for-profit corporation, they provide services and dogs and placed over 8,000 of them into new and loving homes. Statewide, the Humane Society of Missouri has 135 employees, 350 volunteers and dispatch operators who handle up to 1,500 incoming calls every day. Their nine full-time and six part-time veterinarians handle more than 81,000 patients every year, which in-

The Humane Society of Missouri is the fifth oldest humane society in the United States. In 1996, they placed over 8000 dogs into new and loving homes.

programs to the community without one cent of local, state or federal tax support, nor any United Way funding.

As a preeminent animal welfare facility their statistics are staggering: in 1996 the Macklind Avenue site alone received over 21,500 cludes 17,000 surgeries and 10,000 spay/neuters.

Through their nationally recognized Docent volunteer program, over 45,000 St. Louis area children have learned the importance of treating all living things with kindness and respect. The Docent goals in the new facility include new education programs to target all age groups and a partnership program with St. Louis city schools. The future of our animals rests with the next generation of adults.

Karen Patterson hugs her chosen Chow-mix puppy in the get-acquainted room at the Humane Society of Missouri.

The Humane Society has witnessed some changes in their canine population over the past few years; purebred dogs are now about 40 percent, up from the customary 25 percent. Sue Gray, Director of Adoption Services, says that most purebred owner turn-ins arrive at about three months old, with behavior problems as the most commonly cited reason. We're back to the education issue once again.

When a dog is accepted into the center from its owner, it's placed on a 24-hour hold, then goes through a health and temperament screening process and becomes available (hopefully) for adoption. Strays who arrive through animal control or other sources are held five days, examined on day six, then held for 24 hours and turned into the general adoption population. All dogs accepted receive a distemper-parvo combination shot, are vaccinated against Bordetella, tested for heartworm and other internal parasites and flea-dipped if necessary. While the state of Missouri mandates a 72-hour hold on all strays, the humane society has no set holding period for adoption; the time usually depends on available space and the health and temperament of the dog.

When clients first come to the center to adopt a dog, they go through the dog rooms—one for puppies, and one each for adult males and females. If they decide on a dog or puppy, they take the animal into the get acquainted room to visit and complete the adoption questionnaire.

Certain questions are designed as "red flags" to warn the staff to look more closely at the client and the care the animal will receive. The staff always prefers to educate and work with the client. In many cases the adopter simply doesn't understand why a dog should not be chained, why a fence is necessary, why annual vaccinations are a must. If the client refuses to cooperate, he will be denied a dog. In some cases, the staff requires proof that a fence has been erected or will send an investigator to the home before releasing an animal to a questionable situation.

One big question involves the landlord or a relative living with the potential adopter. The staff always calls those people for approval. If none is forthcoming, neither is the dog.

The staff also counsels clients on the dominance factors in some dogs and will do some puppy testing and subordination exercises, especially if the client has young children.

With strict adoption criteria, the return rate on dogs is about seven percent and dropping due to the emphasis on client education. Their new facility will allow them to reach beyond their current education efforts.

In 1988 the Humane Society of Missouri expanded to include the fostering of abused farm-type animals: cows, goats, pigs and other non-domestic critters. Packwood Longmeadow Farm, a 165-acre facility in Union, Missouri, allows these mistreated animals a dignified rehabilitation while awaiting foster care placement and adoption.

Children should be an integral part of the adoption process. This little girl has found a pup she really likes!

BREED RESCUE

In 1996 the American Kennel Club had record of 126 National Breed Club Rescue Networks in the United States. That triple-digit number is one more sad commentary on the fate of purebred dogs in today's high-speed society.

While smaller breeds most frequently populate many puppymills and pet shops, then often end up in animal shelters, small-breed rescues handle fewer adoptions than larger breed groups. The Yorkshire Terrier Club of America is typical of many smaller breed clubs and says that only 15 or 20 Yorkies are placed annually through the National Club due to the fact that when small purebreds end up in shelters, they are usually adopted quickly due to the demand and popularity of small pets.

Greyhound Rescue and Adoption

Greyhound rescue is by far the largest purebred adoption operation in the United States. The national figures are staggering: over 16,000 Greyhounds adopted in 1995, over 14,000 euthanized that year. While those numbers may seem appalling, consider that in 1990 only 3,500 Greyhounds were adopted. A quick calculation will tell you how many more were put to sleep that year.

Greyhound "haul" coordinator Cindy Cash is one of several Greyhound devotees who coordinate Greyhound adoptions across the United States. Whenever a Greyhound racetrack closes permanently or temporarily for the season, Cindy pairs the "retired" racing dogs with adoption groups, then enlists professional

Scotti, a Shetland Sheepdog, was taken to the veterinarian to be euthanized because he was "inconvenient." After convincing the owners to allow him, the veterinarian called the local Shetland Sheepdog rescue committee and Scotti was adopted by Barbara Riley. He poses here with his adopted siblings, Kimmie and Candy.

Volunteers of the Houston chapter of Greyhound Pets of America with a group of retired racers transported when the racetrack in Juarez, Mexico closed abruptly in January, 1996.

haulers who drive the dogs to new locations for foster home placement or adoption.

Greyhound "hauls" often take the drivers (always teams of two) thousands of miles across many state lines, with drop sites from Texas or Florida through Oklahoma, Missouri, Indiana and beyond into the East Coast or western states. It's not uncommon for 50 to 75 Greyhounds to travel en masse, with specific groups of dogs delivered to adoption groups at specific drop-off points. Cindy often "color-codes" the dogs to eliminate confusion and ensure getting the right dog to the right destination: the orange-collar dogs get off in St. Louis, the blue collars go on to Chicago, etc.

Cindy earns high marks from track owners, haulers and adoption groups. Coordinating Greyhound hauls is a nightmare job that requires nerves of steel and a heart that never tires of breaking.

A landscape artist in Baton Rouge, LA, Cindy is part of Greyhound Pets of America, which is the nation's largest national adoption network, but she works with all reliable Greyhound groups. Over a two-year period, she has arranged relocation and rehoming for over 2,000 Greyhounds across the country.

Like most haul coordinators, Cindy tries to move the dogs to metropolitan areas such as Chicago where there are no Greyhound tracks and therefore offer greater adoption potential. (About

35 percent of all Greyhound racers are in the state of Florida.) She also tries to divide the dogs by sex and color so each rescue location will receive a variety of dogs to place. Cindy tries to profile the dogs who will be arriving to give the rescue groups some idea of what kind of dogs will be available. She also works hard to fill specific needs, as when a rescue group has an adoption request for a "quiet black male" or a "smaller brindle female."

Sandy Snyman is one of Cindy's haulers and best known as Greyhound Granny. At almost 60 years old, Sandy drives 100,000 miles cross-country every year delivering retired racing Greyhounds to be rehomed through rescue groups. Sandy works closely with Cindy to plan her routes and destinations whenever dogs become available.

Sandy runs the Greyhound adoption center for Greyhound Pets of America at the Daytona Beach Kennel Club Racetrack, and her office is on the racetrack grounds. Her adoptions are not limited to only GPA rescues, however, and she takes Greyhounds in from anywhere and everywhere, including other racetracks and the local humane society.

Sugar and Spice, former racers named Vixen and Ethyl, now live the good life in Harrisburg, PA, thanks to Cindy Cash. "Greyhounds are the best-kept secret in dogdom, but to save them we need public education," Cindy says.

The Daytona Beach racetrack has 22 kennel buildings, with 50 to 60 Greyhounds in each building. Sandy's adoption center usually has about 30 dogs available for adoption, although she has housed up to 50 at one time. Some of those dogs are adopted by local residents, a few by tourists who come through the area, but most travel with Greyhound Granny to other states for adoption through local rescue groups. Sandy drives an extended cab pickup truck with a ten-hole dog box on the back and pulls an extra-large 10-hole trailer that can hold two to three dogs per hole. Like Cindy Cash, she gets her dogs when Florida racetracks close seasonally or permanently. Because she is always willing to carry a limited number of dogs even if a full load isn't available, Greyhound Granny goes where other haulers won't...places that may be sparsely populated, have limited highway access or are otherwise undesirable. But if there's a Greyhound rescue group waiting for dogs, the Greyhound Granny gets there.

When Sandy hits the road with her Greyhounds, every dog already has a home or an adoption group ready to accept the dog. Each dog has been spayed or neutered, has had its shots and heartworm check, has been wormed for parasites and has had its teeth cleaned and fluoride treated. The rescue groups reimburse her expenses. As with many purebred rescue operations, personal out-of-pocket expense is just a fact of rescue life.

Quincy, IL veterinarian Joanne Klingele and her Racers Recycled rescue operation is frequently on Sandy's rescue route. Over a four-year period Joanne has accepted over 70 Greyhounds from Cindy Cash, Greyhound Granny and other Greyhound adoption groups who had dogs who desperately needed placement. Joanne performs a complete veterinary work-up on each dog, completes their shots, heartworm and parasite testing, spays or neuters and cleans their teeth. She socializes the dogs and evaluates each personality to match them appropriately with their new adoptive families. Occasionally she keeps one or more for longer-term rehabilitation before they go into their new homes. Joanne's

When not sleeping on the sofa or performing at a local coursing event, Minnie Mouse enjoys a stroll along the Panama City beachfront. She formerly raced at Ebro, FL.

Veterinarian Joanne Klingele with 18-month-old "Racers Recycled" Greyhound, Candy, who was "graded out" of the racing program because she didn't meet racing standards.

dedication to the rescue effort stems from her first racing Greyhound encounter with Reno Man and Tara, who immediately "raced" into her heart and became her personal companion dogs.

There are about 30 Greyhound adoption groups in the United States. Many are local groups who operate within a small geographic region. Others have several chapters nationwide and can refer interested parties to the nearest chapter. Several of the larger groups are listed here.

Greyhound Pets of America
(31 chapters)
   Gloria Sanders, 800-FON-1-GPA
Greyhound Club of America
   Cheryl Reynolds
   4280 Carpenteria Dr.
   Carpenteria, CA 93013

Retired Greyhounds as Pets (REGAP)
   Ron Walsek
   P.O. Box 41307
   St. Petersburg, FL 33743
   National Greyhound Network
   415-851-7812
National Greyhound Association (racing organization and industry)
   R.R.3, Box 111B
   Abilene, KS 67410
National Greyhound Adoption Program, Inc.
   8301 Torredale Ave.
   Philadelphia, PA 19136
   David Woolf, 800-348-5217

Golden Retriever Rescue
   The Golden Retriever Club of America has over 30 active rescue groups that work within their member club framework. These

Buddy was found running loose at a local airport and turned in to the humane society. Through the humane society, the author, and the Golden Retriever Club of Greater St. Louis Rescue program, Buddy found a special home with three children who adore him.

dedicated Golden lovers annually rescue thousands of Goldens from animal shelters, owner turn-ins and random pick-ups from the strects and other sources. Like most breed rescue folks, these people dig deep into their personal time and often their pocketbooks, working for the welfare and betterment of the breed they so love.

Golden Retriever Club of America (about 45 rescue services)

Tom Congleton / Arizona, 602-596-9293

Akita Rescue

Nancy Baun of Hawthorne, New Jersey, heads up ARMAC, the Akita Rescue Mid-Atlantic Coast, Inc., for the Akita Club of America. ARMAC is quite blunt in their rescue statement that "Akitas are not for everyone!" A *44-page* rescue packet provides detailed information about the breed and protectively emphasizes the negative side, i.e., that this noble breed is extremely domi-

Sam was turned over to the author by his owner at under two years of age because he fought with their other dog. His new owners think he is the best and smartest dog they've ever owned.

Britta had been thrown from a moving car when she was about five months old and was taken to the Quincy Animal Shelter. Blessed with a loving temperament, she was adopted by Sandy Gilbert.

Rottweiler Rescue

For the past several years Rottweilers have numbered in the top five most popular breeds registered with AKC. Such popularity is never good news for any breed, since it always leads to indiscriminate breeding and breed deterioration. As a large, imposing, guard dog breed, Rottweilers have suffered relentlessly at the hands of unscrupulous breeders and buyers. Rescue volunteers routinely rescue Rottweilers from horror situations. The fact that so many of these gentle giants rehome successfully is testimony to their loving and tenacious spirit.

American Rottweiler Club
Sandra Gilbert, 2060 Vermont, Quincy IL 62301, 217-222-5541

nant and if you fail the dog's first challenge, you will not wish to live with him. These cuddly teddy-bear puppies grow rapidly into aggressive adults who are still used in Japan to hunt bear and wild boar. Akita Rescue urges potential owners to seriously research the breed to prevent another Akita ending up as a shelter or rescue statistic.

Akita Rescue Mid-Atlantic Coast, Inc. (ARMAC)

Nancy Baun, 30 Frederick Ave., Hawthorne NJ 07506

(201) 427-5985

Belinda Lang (914) 223-3132 (Poughkeepsie NY area)

Puller Lanigan (301) 946-3779 (Maryland / Virginia)

Betty McDade (703) 524-9163 (Northern Virginia)

Jodi Marcus (703) 730-0844 (Virginia area)

She was called Flora of the Flood; she arrived at the shelter in Columbia, MO, during the Great Flood of 1993. She was adopted by the Gilbert family and has since passed her CGC test and is a registered Therapy Dog.

Joann Menke, her adopted Australian Shepherd Tia and her foster dog Doc entertain Dandy, an Australian Shepherd-mix.

Australian Shepherd Rescue

Joann Menke covers a four-state area in the Midwest rescuing her beloved Australian Shepherds. In addition to her two personal dogs, Australian Shepherd, Tia, and a German Shepherd friend, it's not unusual for Joann to provide foster care for three or four dogs from the animal shelter or local veterinarians. Some dogs find homes quickly, others may stay a year or more. Makes no difference to Joann...she just loves them all.

Australian Shepherd Club of America Rescue Service

Kyle Kimberly Clarke (800-892-ASCA)

Joann Menke (816/462-3292)

To contact a particular breed rescue service, call or write to the American Kennel Club, 51 Madison Ave., New York NY 10010, 212-696-8231.

A FEW GOOD FOLKS...AND DOGS

Unfortunately too few people seek the services of rescue groups or even shelters. It's easier to dump their dog along a rural highway, drop him off at an interstate rest area, or leave him tied to a tree in the park. Many of the people who abandon their dogs for frivolous or irresponsible reasons don't want to confront their guilt or admit their failure to the shelter or the rescue person. It's easier to hope or pretend someone will find the dog. And after all, it *is* only a dog!

However, not all people who relinquish their dogs are callous or unfeeling. Unexpected changes usually ideal candidates for a great adopted dog.

Most shelters try their level best to evaluate every dog admitted to determine its potential for adoption. Their efforts depend on the time and money available, so some shelters have the luxury of interacting more frequently or intimately with their canine charges. The amount and quality of the time they spend with the dogs determines what kind of

The WGEM Pet of the Week. Each week the television station in Quincy, IL, features a new adoptive pet. Their track record is 100 percent!

may force a family to give up their beloved dog. Children become allergic to dog dander, a parent falls seriously ill, loses his or her job, or is transferred overseas where there is a six-month quarantine on dogs. These dogs are opinion they can offer on their disposition and behavior. Many shelters will hold a dog beyond the required holding period depending on the dog's health, disposition and how the dog presents itself to the public.

DOG ADOPTION GOES HIGH-TECH

Pets have become a major presence on the information superhighway with the arrival of a proliferation of internet resources for people who are considering pet adoption. Many breed clubs, rescue organizations, humane societies, and animal shelters have web sites that give information about the organizations and descriptions of the pets that are available for adoption. These sites are updated regularly, some even daily, to stay current. The amount of information out there can be somewhat overwhelming, so it's best to have time and patience when "surfing the 'net" for a pet. There are a few different ways to begin your search.

If you have a specific breed in mind, accessing the national breed club's site will provide you with breed rescue information or will provide you with a link to the breed rescue's site. You can access the national club or the breed rescue directly if you know their web address, but if you do not, entering the breed's name into the search engine will generate a link through which you can directly access the club's home page. If the national breed club is not online, you should still be able to find some type of regional or local organization. Searching for a specific breed will also generate a list of related sites, one of which may link you directly to the breed rescue.

If you are looking for shelters and humane societies in your area, searching for "pets and adoption," "SPCA," or a related term will generate a list of shelters and pet adoption agencies that have web sites, and you can access whichever ones interest you.

There are also online pet "locator" services that will search their databases for a particular type of dog (or other type of pet) according to the criteria that you input, and if there are any dogs that meet your criteria, will give you the locations where this type of dog is available for adoption. Some of these services are nationwide, such as Mercy Rescue Net (www.aaarf.org) and Doggy Paws (www.doggypaws.com/), and others cover more localized areas, like the New Jersey-based Petfinder (www.petfinder.org).

You may be able to find some information by checking the dog-related chat rooms and message boards on the online service that you use. Some people use the message boards as "classifieds" to list dogs that need new homes, and the dog lovers that you can meet in chat rooms may be able to share some valuable advice with you.

Whatever you choose, you will find that many of these online resources are not just informative, but fun. In addition to dog adoption information, some also offer pet-related merchandise, give information about boarding kennels and grooming, invite visitors to share their pet adoption stories, etc. The possibilities are almost endless, and who knows— you may end up with a new four-legged friend!

Pre-Adoption Homework: Purebred vs. Mixed Breed

If you're hoping to adopt the "perfect" dog (and none will be, but he'll love you so much you'll think he is), do your research first. Learn all you can about the breeds or breed combinations you're considering. Ask your veterinarian, or a friend's veterinarian, what breed(s) he or she would recommend for your family and lifestyle. The source of your adopted dog, whether breeder, breed rescue or a shelter, should be able to explain breed differences and help match you with a suitable companion. There are also excellent books on canine personality and pet selection available in pet stores or advertised in dog magazines. Read them. Take in a dog show and talk to the owners of breeds that interest you. If you're considering a mixed breed pup or adult, knowledge about different breed characteristics will make it easier

Loner, a stray adopted by Bernadette Postle. He wandered onto Bernadette's property, a frightened and skittish six-month-old looking for a handout. After months of gentle coaxing, Loner finally agreed to be "her" dog.

to select a dog since many will carry obvious and predictable qualities from their ancestors. If the mother of a litter is a pure-bred, you'll have at least half an idea about what the pups will look and perhaps act like.

While a purebred dog is more predictable in appearance and personality, the overbreeding of many popular breeds has led to severe health problems in many of those purebreds. Mixed breed dogs are often healthier because nature has provided for their very survival over generations. This process of natural selection is called hybrid vigor, which is a heartiness attributed to cross-breeding in canines. Mixed breeds simply aren't as prone to hip

Cheby, a "pound pup" adopted by Brad and Cheryl Burghart. Cheby has a lot of character, which includes his stubby little tail.

Sheba, a purebred Shiba Inu, was rescued by Jim Icenogle. Today, even the lesser known breeds have their throw-aways.

dysplasia, heart and eye problems or other inherited diseases that are rampant among purebred dogs. Purebred or mixed breed, either choice, do your homework. Unfortunately many people re-search their automobiles far more than they do their dogs, even though the animal will live in the house and be with them for many more years than their vehicle.

Research your potential dog source as well as your dog. Ask your veterinarian, friends and neighbors which animal shelters they would recommend. If you're considering a purebred dog, those shelters who work closely with breed rescue groups or individu-als will gladly refer you to your breed person of choice.

The Westerhoffs

Sally and Tom Westerhoff have been adopting dogs since 1983. Sally finds them everywhere: the animal shelter ("I keep falling in love!"); a mutt rescued from an abandoned trailer ("it took weeks of twice daily feeding just to catch her"); a puppy from a litter that was dumped outside to fend for themselves ("I could write a book about all the clever things she does!"); an abused and lonely Collie, skinny and filthy, who came to the house dragging his chain behind; dogs left behind at the veterinarian kennel—Sally keeps them all. Many of the dogs have required extensive care and surgeries but Sally considers that just another family expense. Tom jokes that all their dogs are grand dogs; they cost about a grand apiece!

"People are always amazed that we have nine dogs," Sally says. "Sometimes I am too! They can't believe we let them come in and share the house with us. Our dogs are truly spoiled but they have spoiled us even more with their unconditional love." Sally's greatest compliment was from a friend who visited at Christmastime. "I hope when I die I'm reincarnated as a Westerhoff dog!"

Dr. Tom and Sally Westerhoff, son Charlie, and their nine adopted canine kids: Sarge, Crockett, Rommel, Hank, Sleepy, Sissy, Shyann, Koko, and Pepper.

Should You Adopt a Dog?

Over 75 percent of shelter dogs are under the age of six months—so there are plenty of puppies looking for good homes like yours!

So why should you adopt a dog from a shelter or a rescue group? Why not buy a pup from a breeder or a neighbor who plans to have puppies sometime soon?

YOU CAN SAVE A DOG

Most people who adopt their pets do so because they care about dogdom and feel they're contributing to the war against pet overpopulation by saving a dog from euthanasia. One shelter statistic reveals that each year a shelter dog is euthanized every 6.7 seconds. That's not surprising when another statistic estimates that in the United States over 2,000 puppies are born every hour compared to 415 human beings.

DOGS OF ALL AGES

If you're concerned about finding a shelter filled with mostly older dogs, shelter figures also show that over 75 percent of adopted shelter dogs are younger than six months of age and that only 16 percent of dogs are over one year old when acquired. Good news for young dog advocates!

Some older dogs in shelters already have been spayed or neutered and most make great, loving pets.

SHELTER ADVOCATES

Ask anyone who has adopted a dog from a rescue or a shelter, and they'll agree..."This is the best dog we ever had...the best thing we ever did...he's like one of our children...we were made for each other." If you're thinking "new dog" and you've never visited a shelter, now's the time. You'll be amazed at the many fine dogs who are housed there. Most of them have the potential to become a sterling member of a family that is properly matched to their size and personality.

Dogs who have been abandoned or mistreated usually bond eagerly with a human "pack leader" who offers them attention and loving care. It may take a while, especially with dogs who have been seriously abused, but your rehabilitated dog will love you unconditionally for life, which is the ultimate bonus of owning a dog.

COST

Another obvious advantage of adoption is the initial cost. Although adoption fees vary, the cost is still less than the purchase price of a purebred pup. Most of the older dogs often have updated shots and may already be spayed or neutered, while puppies will need a complete battery of shots and early veterinary care. However, don't confuse the reduced initial cost with the lifetime expense of owning the dog.

Belle is Floyd Ginster's second adopted shelter dog. She was perfect from the start—housebroken and well trained!

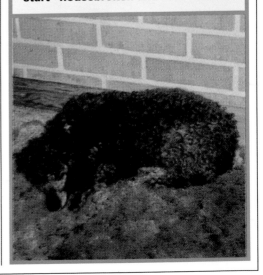

SHOULD YOU *OWN* A DOG?

While you're debating your decision to adopt, you should also examine the reasons why you want a dog in the first place and what kind of dog you're looking for. You want to be sure your dog doesn't end up back at the shelter because you led with your heart and not your brain. There are important questions to ask—and honestly answer—before making the commitment to adopt a dog.

Time

Will a dog fit into your busy schedule; do you have enough time? This is one of the major reasons owners give up their pets, and for the animal's sake, you don't want history to repeat itself.

Most breeds, or combinations of breeds, have different exercise requirements, with some needing plenty of heavy-duty playtime or they will redirect their energy into creative mischief. (Yards are for digging holes, furniture is to chew on, etc.) You must allow lots of time to exercise your dog, take it to obedience class, teach it basic house manners, then make sure you have the time to maintain those courtesies. (Yes, dogs need routine reminders and reinforcement just like children do. It's like living with a five-year-old for life.)

Space

Will your living quarters best accommodate a large or small animal? A large dog requires more

Most breeds have different characteristics and therefore different requirements. Longhaired dogs, like Scotti, need extensive grooming. Will you have time for this?

space and exercise and should have a fenced backyard. Smaller dogs are more popular and more acceptable in apartments or condominiums. (Think Great Dane on the 18th floor.) If you rent or live in a multiple-family dwelling, be sure you have written permission to bring a dog into your building or complex and that you understand any restrictions that apply; special potty and exercise areas or times and poop scooping rules (a must if your dog is to remain welcome).

Budget

Can you afford to own a dog? Like children, dogs need more than love. Food, veterinary care, training classes, registration fees, grooming, miscellaneous items and probable pest control make up a hefty canine expense account. Based on an 11-year lifespan, and depending on the animal's size ("large" costs more to feed and outfit), the average dog will cost at least $500 a year for food, medical attention and other costs plus grooming if you

own a breed that may require professional care, and up to $11,000 during its lifetime. And that doesn't include the initial cost of the dog from a breeder, rescue or animal shelter. If your budget is already stretched, maybe you should think about getting a hamster.

Before you adopt a dog, make sure you can afford it. Ellie, a seven-year-old Beagle, was abandoned at the veterinarian's because her owner decided she wasn't worth paying the bill. She was adopted by Kristen Kanoy and is a perfect companion for Kristen's nephew, Ben.

Dog Hair

Will dog hair drive you crazy? Most dogs shed, some more than others. Certain long-haired breeds require extra time for extensive grooming to keep their long coats free of mats and tangles. (When a heavy or double-coated breed sheds its winter coat, you'll wear out your brushing arm.) Will you have time to do it? Can you afford a groomer? If dog hair on your suit or sofa is unacceptable, consider a non-shedding breed. However, those few dogs who don't shed must be groomed regularly or their coats become seriously matted, so be sure you can afford professional services for coat care.

Selection: What Kind of Dog Should You Adopt?

COMPANION DOG

Do you want a family companion for your children or an aging parent? If your kids are active or rambunctious, always climbing trees and playing tag football, consider a dog or breed who would happily join such activities without being intimidated or even hurt. A shy or quiet child might be happier with a smaller or less active dog. An elderly person may prefer a couch-potato pooch who is willing to lounge in front of the TV much of the day. Are you a hunter, a sailor, a hiker? Do you jog and dream of four furry feet running at your side? What about dog shows or other forms of canine competition?

Your lifestyle and interests are an important barometer in your decision to adopt a dog and what type or breed you choose.

WATCHDOG

Are you looking for a watchdog or a guard dog who will make you

If you are fond of the Great Outdoors, you might want to consider adopting one of the sporting dogs—like a Golden Retriever.

Take me home—I'll be your best friend.

feel safe or more secure? Most dogs can be trained to bark at a strange noise or signal the approach of a stranger or intruder. However, adopting a large breed known for its aggressive tendencies would present serious training problems for the average or novice dog owner. Few people are experienced enough to train or control a dog who is naturally prone to growl or attack strangers. Without expert control, such an animal also could threaten the safety of your own family and friends. Further, many popular guard dog breeds are at the shelter because their owners failed to train them properly and were unable to control them. Reversing those tendencies could be difficult to impossible. Such aggressiveness should be dealt with only by professionals who have experience in attack and guard dog training.

PUPPY OR OLDER DOG

When you adopt a dog who has grown beyond the cute puppy stage, what you see is what you get. This dog will not surprise you by growing up...and up... beyond your wildest dreams. You can predict the coat and size, and often the personality, of a dog who has outgrown puppyhood. An older or more mature dog may be housebroken and have some degree of basic house manners. Puppies are great fun, but they are work, frustrating work, and you can bypass that struggle with a dog who's outgrown the aggravations of adolescence.

Puppy Research—Books, Books, Books

However, if you still prefer a puppy, you should first read a good book on puppy rearing before you start your puppy search. Most puppy books include some simple exercises for puppy testing so you can discover the personality under all that fuzzy fur. The rest of the book will be a valuable resource and daily reference in dealing with a puppy's first six to 12 months.

Shelter policies vary about puppy raising with some agencies farming litters out to foster homes until the pups reach five or six weeks of age.

Puppies need socialization with humans. Katherine McGowan, publicity director for the Humane Society of Missouri, gets hugs and kisses.

Before you add a puppy to your family, read a book on puppy rearing such as *A New Owner's Guide to Training the Perfect Puppy* by Andrew DePrisco and published by TFH Publications, Inc.

Socialized Puppies

Whether pups are shelter-raised from birth or reared with foster parents, socialization with people and a varied environment is critical between six and 16 weeks of age. A pup who is housed alone during that period will have difficulty adjusting to the outside world. A puppy must be taken out of his kennel frequently to experience new environments or kennel shyness will result. He must spend time alone with humans at least 15 minutes every day or he'll be socially retarded. Such a puppy will have difficulty adjusting to people and may remain suspicious or frightened of anything new or different or be highly excitable when exposed to unfamiliar things. The "hyper" dog, one who "freaks out," trembles in fear and urinates, is often a product of zero to poor socialization. Make proper or at least adequate socialization a primary consideration in your puppy selection process.

A Healthy Pup

Health is of course a major concern when adopting a dog of any age. Puppies especially are vulnerable to all forms of canine disease throughout their first 16-to-20-weeks. Even puppies who have been vaccinated can contract a disease if the natural immunities from their mother overrode the care as a pup. Dogs of all ages should be checked for heartworm before they are adopted.

Puppy Selection

Be sure to enlist the help of shelter personnel if you decide to adopt a puppy. Personalities emerge at a very early age, and the staff can help you select a

Puppies are especially vulnerable to all forms of canine disease throughout their first 20 weeks of life. Proper vaccinations are essential.

vaccine. Stray dogs admitted to the shelter often bring in parasites or viruses, many of which are airborne and can easily infect a pup. Your shelter puppy should be wormed, checked for fleas and other external parasites and have been vaccinated every two to three weeks. Adult dogs should also have received the same preventive health well-balanced pup who is neither too dominant nor too insecure. They can also offer experienced opinions on the breed mix and potential size, although that's no guarantee. The pup with huge paws may never grow beyond 40 pounds, while a runt of a pup might be a fooler and double or triple his predicted weight.

Devil Dog

Devil Dog" was turned in to the animal shelter as a vicious dog. When Rottweiler rescue coordinator Sandy Gilbert was called to evaluate his temperament, she found a rather boisterous 10-month-old puppy who was untrained, afraid of almost everything, and was seriously underweight with welts, healing abrasions and lacerations and scars all over his body. Sandy took him home, renamed him Karl Freimachen (translation: Karl liberated from jail), and slowly nurtured him into a happy, outgoing, cart-pulling, registered therapy dog who visits nursing homes and enjoys getting mushed on by the old folks.

"Devil Dog"

"Hoss"

Hoss

Hoss, a Great Dane, was removed from his owner by animal control authorities because of severe cruelty and abuse. He had cigarette burns on his belly, a big lump on his head and was half his normal weight. In fact, Hoss actually ran away from his owner and up to the animal control warden's truck, as if saying, "Please take me away!" His disposition was so exceptionally sweet the shelter decided to nurse him back to health. Despite the extreme abuse, the big dog never held a grudge and loved everyone he met. He was adopted by Walid Hafez. He lives the good life now and accompanies his mistress everywhere.

Shelter Policies and Adoption: The Process

Shelter staff member during "cuddle-puppy" duty.

Okay, you've passed all the canine conditions and requirements. It's time to find your dog. First resolve to make several visits to several shelters as insurance for your adoption screening process. Your veterinarian should be able to refer you to at least one reliable shelter. The best source for a novice dog owner is a well-established shelter operated by experienced and knowledgeable people. Size isn't as important as the manner in which the shelter is managed. Large or small, it should look "maintained" and as clean as any multiple-dog confinement facility can look, considering the habits of dogs. The dogs should appear well-cared for and the staff should be caring and concerned about the animals housed there.

Shelters usually operate with limited funds and many rely on volunteer help to supplement their very existence. Thus some are better than others, more efficient, knowledgeable and more particular in their care for the animals as well as for the people who might adopt them.

The actual adoption process will vary according to the policies of each shelter or rescue organization. Both agencies will ask about your history with previous dogs, if you have a house or an apartment, whether the dog will be left alone all day, plus other personal and canine information. That's good. The more they ask, the more they care.

You will fill out questionnaires, sometimes during your initial inquiry, and/or again when you receive the dog. Typical forms ask for specifics about your circumstances and living situation. Do you have children, their ages, a fenced yard, own or rent? Where will your pet be housed, both day and night? (Many shelters and all rescues will refuse to place a dog if it will live on a chain in the yard, although they do their best to educate clients on why this is unacceptable and work toward a solution.) How do you plan to care for the dog—exercise, housebreak, train, groom, health care? What's your dog history, have you owned a dog before and what happened to it or them? (If previous dogs were hit by cars or some other careless tragedy befell them, especially at an early age, shelters will seriously question and explore those circumstances before they release a dog.) If the client is adamant and refuses the educational efforts of the staff, he may be denied an animal.

If you own or have owned other dogs, you'll need to provide veterinary references. Responsible shelters always follow up and call the named veterinarian to verify the animals have had proper health care. They often discover the vet never saw the dog in question.

Some shelters require written permission from a landlord if you live in a rental unit. Many shelters

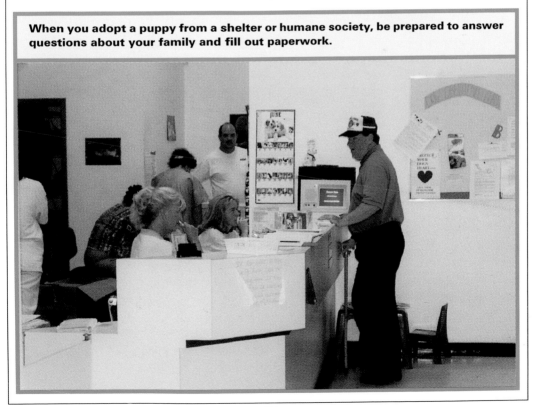

When you adopt a puppy from a shelter or humane society, be prepared to answer questions about your family and fill out paperwork.

Many shelters waive the adoption fees for seniors, as studies have shown that seniors take better care of their pets.

only a parvo and rabies shot and require the family to follow up with a more complete health exam and vaccinations. Each agency operates according to the funds available, which can seriously limit the health care of their canine charges.

Since most rescue dogs live in foster care with other dogs, they are usually fully vaccinated before being adopted. Rescue adoption fees range up to $100. Most organizations and shelters agree if you can't afford the adoption fee, you can't afford to own a dog.

PETS FOR SENIORS

Senior citizens are the exception. Many shelters waive the adoption fees for seniors as a community service. Occasionally area veterinarians also offer special pet care rates to seniors. These contributions are due to the many studies that have proven that pets are a potent anti-aging tonic for the elderly. Seniors who own dogs are more active, have lower blood pressure, make fewer trips to the doctor, suffer less depression and make friends more easily. Pets also provide seniors with a sense of security. Studies also have shown that seniors take better care of their pets and better care of themselves. (Of course these are all the same great reasons why people of any age should own a dog.)

SPAY/NEUTER

If the dog you choose is still intact, you can expect a spay/neuter agreement as a pre-condition to the adoption. Many shel-

and almost all rescues want to meet all members of the family before approving an adoption. The more detailed the screening process, the better chance that the dog's rehoming will be permanent and successful. The last thing shelters and rescues want is a dog that bounces from one home to another, subjected to all the stress involved with every relocation.

Some shelters provide a complete battery of shots before releasing a dog. Others may give ters won't relinquish a dog until after it is altered. Others offer a special rate for the surgery, and you may be required to show proof after the dog has been altered.

Rescue groups always insist on spaying/neutering. And for good reason. Most of the dogs they care for are the result of irresponsible breedings and their fate could have been averted had the sire and dam been unable to reproduce. Most groups alter their dogs before placing them rather than risk a new owner's failure to do so. A few require follow-up proof of alteration and will not hesitate to reclaim a dog if the family doesn't follow through.

The spay/neuter process is good for the dog as well as the dog population. Females spayed before their first heat cycle will never suffer from uterine or ovarian cancer, a common killer of unspayed bitches, nor will they contract pyometra, a life-threatening disease of the uterus that occurs most frequently in intact females over six years of age. Your female will be cleaner without the mess of estrus fluids, you won't have amorous males lurking about your yard, and your little girl will never miss having that litter of pups.

Nor will your male dog miss the fun either. Early neutering not only prevents testicular and other male cancers, it also eliminates the urge to roam in search of romance (he does not need that to fulfill his heritage!) and reduces aggressive tendencies toward other male dogs.

Contrary to popular belief, spaying/neutering does not make a dog fat. Only too much food or too little exercise produces chubby dogs. Spay/neuter is the best gift you can give your dog...and the dog world.

Doggie decor at the Quincy Humane Society.

Dog Shopping

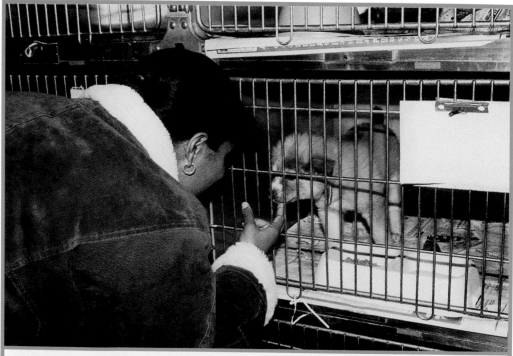

Puppy shopping—who can resist such sweet little furries?

Whether your choice is pure-bred or mixed breed, you should discuss your preferences and lifestyle with shelter personnel. Ask questions about different canine characteristics and behaviors. Which of their dogs are owner turn-ins and which ones came in as strays or through animal control? Dogs relinquished by their owners often arrive with their history, which may or may not have been embellished by a well-meaning owner who hopes "good references" will aid in the animal's adoption. Most strays have questionable backgrounds, but responsible shelters use the state-mandated three-to-seven day holding period to evaluate a dog's temperament for soundness and adoption potential. Animals with serious health or behavior problems are of necessity euthanized. Shelters don't want any dog to be reshuffled, and they do their best to place the adoptable ones in good, permanent homes. Their evaluation isn't necessarily a guarantee of a dog's disposition, but it's a good beginning.

If the shelter or rescue person doesn't volunteer a particular dog's history or enough information, ask. Is this dog good with

Please pick me! Shelter dogs beg for attention from potential adopters.

each facility and carefully observe the dogs. Some shelters have history and/or information cards attached to each kennel or run. "Good with children...housebroken...some obedience training." Many facilities have get-acquainted rooms where you can spend time with individual dogs away from the din and incessant barking that fill the kennel areas.

The best bets for adoption are dogs who appear stable and comfortable despite the chaotic kennel atmosphere. While it's true that shelter dogs may exhibit some unusual behaviors because they have been uprooted and are reacting to a stressful kennel environment, a dog who appears shy or cowers in the corner of his space may in reality be a shy or

kids or other dogs, or cats if you happen to own one? If your children are grown, but your grandkids visit, you need to make sure this is a child-friendly animal. Does the dog appear to be housebroken? Is there a particular reason why the dog behaves as he does...jumps constantly, cringes at an outstretched hand, urinates when petted? The more advance information you gather, the better prepared you'll be to select the right dog for you and your family.

GETTING ACQUAINTED
Armed with the shelter's references and observations, it's time for you to evaluate the dogs who seem to fit your future dog's profile. Browse the kennels of

Many shelters have areas outside where you can take the dogs to get better acquainted. This dog is buttering up the prospects with a few kisses.

fearful dog and be difficult to rehabilitate. Avoid any dog who growls, bares his teeth or shows signs of overt aggression toward visitors at his space. The dog may have been abused, be aggressive by nature, or simply be having a bad day, but whatever the reason, he is not a candidate for successful rehoming. Be sure to mention signs of aggression to the shelter staff in case they're unaware of the behavior.

While touring the kennel areas, talk calmly and quietly to the dogs and observe their reaction to your overtures. Look for happy wagging tails; not all wagging postures are friendly signals. How does the dog respond to a calm and friendly outstretched hand? Does the dog stare or raise the hackles on his back? These can be signs of

A serious getting acquainted session at the Humane Society of Missouri.

While touring the kennel areas, observe the dogs' behavior and response to people. This pooch is performing in hopes of winning over a new family.

dominance or suspicion and shouldn't be ignored.

Avoid dogs who appear overly fearful or ones who display signs of submissive urination. Fearful and submissive behaviors may or may not be cured. Also look at the dog's hygiene habits in his run. A dog who eliminates all over his space and then walks through his stools might be difficult to housebreak.

Concentrate only on those dogs who appear friendly and stable. A questionable dog may be worth saving, but are you willing and able to take on that task? Can you subject your family to the problems and the risks involved?

Promise yourself you won't fall in love or make your selection with your heart, unless the dog who steals it is a good candidate for rehoming. Be willing to wait and look again...and again. Try not to feel guilty and take a dog just to save him, as difficult as that may be. The dog must be right for you or he'll just end up back at the shelter.

SIGNS OF POOR HEALTH

While this issue may seem obvious, you should look also for a healthy animal. When evaluating potential adoptees at a shelter or rescue source, be sure the animal appears robust and healthy. Any discharge or foul odor from the dog's eyes, nose or ears, any open sores or scabby areas, a lack of energy or lethargic manner, all are indicators of poor health. A dull dry coat, bloated rib cage, or constant scratching may be a sign of fleas, other internal parasites or allergies. You should discount any animal who appears ill or has suspicious symptoms. Bring those conditions to the attention of shelter personnel.

THE FINAL CHOICE

Once you've narrowed your choices to one or more dogs, ask a shelter worker to accompany you and the dog into the designated visiting area if they offer one. Again, observe the dog and his

"Give me five." Concentrate on the dogs that are friendly and responsive.

It is important during the getting acquainted sessions that children interact and feel comfortable with the dog.

While visiting with each dog under consideration, interact with the dog through play activities. Roll a ball to fetch or toss a squeaky toy. Is the dog happy and playful with you and does he welcome petting and handling? When petted does he shrink away? That's not too bad as long as the dog warms up to you after a few minutes of gentle overtures. Test the dog's response, if any, to "Sit" and "Down" obedience commands. Use food treats as rewards to see if the dog will comply with your requests.

Walk around the room and chat lightly with the dog. Does he follow you, cower or run away? A very nervous dog who shies away may be difficult to rehabilitate. Will he walk willingly on a leash? How does he respond to a light tug to keep him moving along with you? If space prevents you from evaluating the dog in this

comfort level with the shelter staff. How does the dog respond to the shelter person and does he act differently toward you and your family? Often a dog with a dominant personality is polite and well-behaved with authoritative, experienced humans, but will resist control by anyone he senses to be unsure or subordinate. While these are not insurmountable problems, you have to recognize them and be prepared to deal with a dog who might try to take over your house and constantly challenge you for "Top Dog" status.

Does the dog welcome petting and handling? This pup just can't get enough.

manner, you might visit another time or try a different facility.

Certain behaviors should send up a warning flag. You should be aware of them upfront and be prepared to deal with them or look for a different animal. Your adopted dog will be with you for many years; these are just security measures to help to ensure a happy life together.

ADOPTING FROM BREED RESCUE

If you adopt your dog from a breed rescue group, most of this evaluation may have been handled by a foster family. Responsible rescue groups generally place their dogs in foster care for a period of time to evaluate the dog, his temperament and any prior training to determine the best future environment for the dog. A rescue representative interviews prospective adopters in person and with written questionnaires to determine the family's needs and if they would provide a proper loving home for one of

This little girl has found a new home!

their breed. Rescues are usually more stringent in their adoption criteria (fenced yards, family circumstances, etc.), while shelters seldom have the luxury of such selective placement. Rescues sometimes offer a trial period to see if the dog and new family will be compatible. If you decide to adopt through a breed rescue, you should still research the breed to make sure it's right for you. The more knowledgeable you are, the better your chances that the rescue committee will approve you as an adopter and pair you with the right dog. If you haven't already asked all the important questions, be sure to do so before you sign the final paperwork and take your new dog home. You've made a grand decision and you can look forward to many years of loving companionship, especially if you did your pre-adoption homework. The only heartache in adoption is that you can't save them all.

Romeo

When Chris Keane accompanied her boss to the animal shelter to pick up the boss's lost dog, she realized that since her dog had died the previous Christmas, this would be the perfect place to find another dog. She returned the next day, and when she walked past the cages, Romeo stuck his nose through the kennel fencing and looked at her with huge brown eyes. That was it! He was dubbed Romeo because of his loving nature.

When Chris took Romeo home, she discovered he was already housebroken. He was also an instant hit with her husband, son and two cats. "He's here every day to greet us and make us feel good even when we've had a bad day," Chris says. "He's always happy to take us for a walk and asks for nothing in return for the love and loyalty he gives us every day. Even though he has four feet and eats out of a bowl on the floor, he's still considered an important member of our family."

"Romeo"

"Oliver"

Oliver

Dorothy Smith heard about Oliver from the shelter staff who came to her workplace with the Shelter on the Road program. "They told me how sweet he was, so of course I went to see him. Naturally we fell in love! My husband got Oliver for me for our anniversary. Ollie got along fine with our black Lab Shadow. We kept the dogs in different rooms at first, then took them out together the next day. They growled a little but Shadow was alpha and Ollie understood that. At first Ollie wouldn't eat until after Shadow ate. But soon the dogs slept together and played games and tug-of-war with each other. Ollie is great with our children, Amanda and Jarod, loves his tennis ball and plays hide and seek games with the kids.

Thinking Like a Dog

THE COMMUNICATION PROCESS

Before you collect your new dog to begin his "rehab" in your home, you should have a good understanding of canine behavior and the canine thinking process. Of course you know dogs don't rationalize in human terms, but you need to understand how your dog thinks if you're going to communicate successfully with him and teach him the rules of his new home.

You want a good friend, right? And one you can be proud of, one who'll walk tall beside you while people gasp in wonder and say, "Gosh, what a great dog you have." Okay, maybe that's extreme, but it's certainly a worthwhile goal.

To reach that end, you have to master Canine Communication 101. Dogs are very social creatures, pack animals who, thanks to their wolf ancestors, instinctively sense and respond to a

Understanding your dog's body language is important. Celia is looking for a tummy rub.

Communicate in dog terms to teach your dog good manners and the rules of his new home.

pecking order to establish the boundaries in their world. If a dog doesn't know who's in charge, he feels insecure and will always, unconsciously but instinctively, be inching up the ladder to be the boss, the one in charge, because if no one leads, he'll have to assume that position himself. And it's that alpha thing you've read and heard so much about. It's a survival instinct that goes back to the time of Noah. Not much different really than raising children. Someone has to be in charge or chaos reigns. Or runs away. Or maybe even bites.

LIFE IN THE PACK

In the wild, in the pack, every-thing in a canid's life comes after the leader, the alpha dog, is satisfied, has had his fill, or gives permission. Dogs are not un-happy with this arrangement. Rather they feel secure knowing they have a leader who is strong, protects and guards the pack and keeps other pack members in their proper place. So social is their nature, they are happy knowing they have pleased their leader. So too with you and your new dog.

How do you achieve this status as your dog's new pack leader? By communicating in the only way canines understand, through obedience and house training with a firm but loving hand. That process will make him feel safe and confident in his new home.

POSITIVE AND NEGATIVE REINFORCEMENTS

All dogs are learning machines. Some breeds are better students because of their ancestry, but every dog will try to please his leader if the dog is treated with respect and understands what is expected of him. Today's obedience instructors find it's better to train a dog with positive reinforcement instead of the older methods that required hitting, pushing, jerking, and other forms of punishment. Sure, there's a time for gentle discipline, but you first must teach the dog.

Dogs learn best through repetition and reward. Discipline comes only after a dog understands what

Reward good behavior with praise and occasional bits of food treats; such positive reinforcement will encourage your dog to repeat that behavior.

it should and should not do. Using positive reinforcement, lots of "Good dog!" praise and occasional bits of a food treat, good behavior is rewarded, the dog feels good, and so repeats that behavior. It's also true that if the dog does something naughty that is fun or makes him feel good (as in sleeping on the sofa or stealing food) and he gets away with it, even once, he will surely do it again. (Your lesson here is never take your eyes off the dog until he is completely trustworthy.)

BE CONSISTENT

Consistency is the key to success with any method of training. By applying the same word to each desired behavior when it occurs, the dog will soon repeat the action when he hears the command word. This principle applies to puppies as well as adult dogs. By using food or other lures (squeaky toys for example), you can initiate some actions, such as sit and down, and learning will automatically follow. With other behaviors, such as house training, you must wait until the dog performs outside (as he surely will!) and immediately apply the praise.

THE HERE AND NOW

Dogs learn in the present tense. Even seconds later is too late. You can use a correction only if you catch the dog at the exact moment of a naughty deed, such as eliminating on your carpet. Only then will he understand a strong voice correction, "Aaah, Aaah!" or "No!" as you whisk him out the door to where he should be "going." After the act, whatever that act may be, even when a dog knows better, is always too late.

AN OUNCE OF PREVENTION

Preventing mischief before it happens is better than correcting for it, especially if your dog learns a lesson in the process. Example: your dog lingers at the kitchen

newspaper or other object. That will not teach him a thing and will only make him hand-shy and afraid of you. (Please don't confuse fear with respect.) You should also remember that dogs do not understand human anger (grit your teeth...) and will only become confused and frightened. Even a shouting match with your spouse will send him

Your dog will become your child's best friend, the special friend she can share her secrets with.

counter, eyeing the slab of beef you've set out for tonight's dinner. You know what he's thinking about! A stern "Aaahh, aaahh!" will change his mind before the deed is done. Just watch him lower his posture and slip away. You've averted a disaster, and your dog thinks you're a mind reader.

NO HITTING ALLOWED

Never, ever hit your dog with your hand or swat him with a

scurrying...he's sure that he's to blame.

You often hear it said that the dog knew he was naughty because he had a "guilty look" when his owner came home and found the waste basket upturned and spilled. In reality, the dog was reacting to his owner's behavior and connected that anger with the mess on the floor, not the fact that he put it there two hours ago. What's obvious to us often is not clear to the dog.

THE OWNER IS ALPHA

Assuming the role of pack leader is an essential element of training and important in the obedience process. Once the dog has mastered certain lessons, you can use them to reinforce your alpha role. These are valuable disciplinary tools and should be used as reminders that you're the one in charge. The dog jumps up...Whoops!...give a "Sit" command and insist that he sits until released from that position. Be sure to praise him while he's sitting and tell him what a good fellow he is. Make him sit before he gets his food dish, before he goes out the door and as soon as he comes in. Make him "Down-Stay" while you read the paper. Scratch his head for being good, but make him stay. Your assertive body posture, the firm way you pat his chest, all such mannerisms remind your dog that you're the boss and reinforce that secure feeling all dogs need. Just remem-

Hugs and kisses are an important ingredient in puppy praise.

ber, some dogs need reminding more than others.

Never engage in rough housing games with an untrained dog. Power-struggle play activities that invite your dog to challenge your Top Dog status encourage canine aggression, and the last thing you need is an aggressive dog who thinks he's the boss.

Play obedience games instead. Your dog will think you're a fun pal and learn to enjoy obedience in the process. Once he understands "Sit" and "Down," give him "pop quiz" with unexpected commands in a happy voice, a super-quick food reward, a big hug and silly talk. Run the commands together: "Sit"... "Down"... "Sit"... "Down", then a huge "Free!" with hugs and kisses. Act as silly as a puppy; your dog won't tell a soul.

Assertive body posture reminds your pet that you're "top dog." Standing over a dog signals dominance; lower body posture signals submission.

A Visual Guide to
Canine Communication

PLAY-SOLICITING

AGGRESSION

AROUSAL

SUBMISSION

FEAR

Dog Supplies

Make shopping for your new dog a grand adventure. This will be your dog's personal wardrobe. Envision your new dog as you select each item on your list and how much he'll enjoy having his own "stuff." Tailor your purchases to suit your new dog, small sizes for little guys...you know the rest.

Most good quality dog supplies are available in pet stores.

FOOD DISHES OR BOWLS

Two non-tippable, stainless steel or heavy stoneware, one each for food and water. Remember how often you'll have to pick it up when you look at a heavy stoneware bowl that matches your decor. Non-breakable is practical. Plastic is too easily chewed and doesn't sanitize well.

LEASHES

A 4- to 6-foot nylon leash is fine for a young pup, but an older dog will need a 6-foot leather lead, especially in obedience class. Narrow leads, $1/4$-inch wide for a small dog and $1/2$-to-$3/4$-inch wide for a large one. A "flexi-lead," an 8- to 20-foot retractable leash that reels in automatically, is especially handy for exercise in public places.

Your dog should have two bowls, one for food and one for water. Stainless steel bowls are sturdy and sanitary.

COLLARS

Nylon or leather buckle or safety-snap collars work best for most dogs. Rolled leather is often preferred for long-haired breeds, although some leather dyes may stain the fur. Chain or "choke" collars are for training only and never left on the dog at any other time. Most obedience classes recommend chain training collars for the average dog at about six months of age, a little earlier for larger breeds.

IDENTIFICATION TAGS

Proper identification is a must! Avoid ID tags with an "S" hook attachment; they snag carpeting and bedding and easily fall off. Key or "O" ring attachments are more secure. Many sporting dog owners prefer a brass plate ID that is riveted on the collar. Never include the dog's name on his tag; it will allow a thief to call your dog. Some owners include an extra line on the ID tag or plate as an additional precaution: "Dog needs medication," or "Reward" in

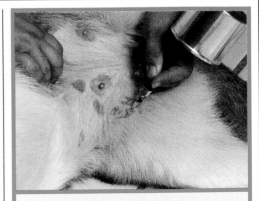

Tattooing is one way to permanently identify your dog. The procedure is not painful for the dog.

hopes of encouraging a lost or stolen dog's swift return.

TATTOOS AND MICROCHIPS

At the earliest time possible, your new dog should also be permanently identified with a tattoo or microchip. Many owners opt for both. Stories abound about dogs who have been returned to their owners because of such identification. The best example lies with the new AKC Companion Animal Recovery program with over 1,700 enrolled

A nylon safety-snap collar is safe and comfortable for your dog.

animals recovered in 1995. Some shelters offer microchip services as do most veterinarians.

GROOMING TOOLS

Brush, comb, nail clippers and shampoo, all selected according to your dog's breed(s) or coat type. A wire brush and comb for long-haired dogs, a bristle brush for shorter coats. A slicker brush also works well on most coats. Your veterinarian, groomer or shelter personnel can help you choose the proper equipment for your individual dog.

Ask your veterinarian to demonstrate the nail clippers during your first visit. Nails should be clipped regularly or you'll have snags and scratches in your house and on yourself. Some dogs

Designed upon the principles of the great Italian inventor Galileo Galilei, who sketched what he believed would be the strongest bone, the Galileo® safely works the teeth and jaws of the most powerful chewer.

Ask your veterinarian to demonstrate using the nail clippers during your first visit.

object to having their feet handled or nails trimmed. If a large dog resists and a struggle ensues, the dog can become distrustful of other handling as well. Pay close attention to how your veterinarian handles the dog during nail trimming. If your dog objects, use treats to form a pleasant association. And you may have to settle for one foot at a time.

TOYS

Of course! These should also be selected specifically for your special dog. All dogs need chew toys, just make sure they're safe...Nylabones®, rope toys such as Nylafloss® (for chewing only, *not* for tugging!), hard rubber balls or hard imitation bones (stuff them with a small dab of peanut butter to keep your dog amused for hours). Most dogs enjoy rawhide chews, but they should be used with supervision to prevent the dog from swallowing too large a chunk and choking. Too many rawhide treats can also cause loose stools and intestinal blockage, so use them with discretion.

A new product, molded rawhide, is very safe. During the process, the rawhide is melted and then injection molded into the familiar dog shape (a bone). It is very hard and eagerly accepted

The Gumabone® Frisbee's™ non-toxic polyurethane construction is built to last—it's a super-strong flying disc, but it's flexible enough to be comfortable for your dog to carry, and the bone on top makes it easy to pick up.

Nylafloss® is a great chew toy. Your dog can retrieve it, and it does wonders for his dental health by massaging his gums and flossing between his teeth, loosening plaque and tartar build-up. Unlike cotton knot toys, Nylafloss® is made with the strongest, safest fibers, which won't rot or fray.

that can be chewed off and swallowed. Woolly stuffed toys are fun, but beware; some dogs shred instead of cuddle.

Give your dog a chew that will promote his well-being—a Nylabone®. It is the only plastic dog bone made of 100% virgin nylon, specially processed to create a tough, durable, completely safe bone.

by all dogs. The melting process also sterilizes the rawhide. Don't confuse this with pressed rawhide, which is nothing more than small strips of rawhide squeezed together.

Be careful of small toys or balls that could be swallowed and squeaky toys with eyes or parts

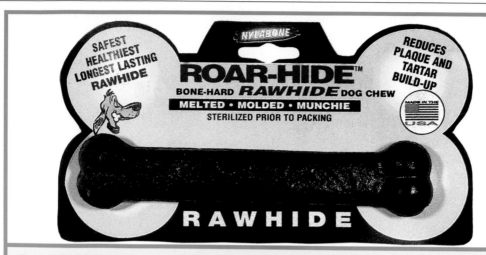

SAFEST
HEALTHIEST
LONGEST LASTING
RAWHIDE

NYLABONE

ROAR-HIDE™
BONE-HARD *RAWHIDE* DOG CHEW
MELTED · MOLDED · MUNCHIE
STERILIZED PRIOR TO PACKING

REDUCES
PLAQUE AND
TARTAR
BUILD-UP

MADE IN THE
USA

R A W H I D E

To combat boredom and relieve your dog's natural desire to chew, there's nothing better than a Roar-Hide®. Unlike common rawhide, this bone won't turn into a gooey mess when chewed on, so your dog won't choke on pieces of it. It is completely edible and high in protein (over 86%) and low in fat (less than $\frac{1}{3}$ of 1%).

When offering all these goodies to your dog, limit his choices to three or four toys at a time. Like children, dogs can become bored with too many toys at once. Rotating his toys will keep his interest peaked.

DOG BEDS

He'll need a sturdy bed of his own and there are many to choose from. Lambswool pads, cushiony cedar bags, wicker baskets, all are comfy and attractive, but some dogs chew them up to relieve their

A lambswool pad makes a warm, soft, and attractive bed for your dog. There are many types of dog beds available at your local pet shop.

stress or boredom. Fiberglass beds lined with blankets or bedding are not very tasty and are fairly indestructible. Initially the dog may shred the bedding material, so it's practical to use an old blanket or heavy towel to line a bed or crate.

DOG LIBRARY

Build a canine library with books that focus on specific issues like puppy and obedience training, canine health, first aid and emergency care. New videos on canine care and training have become popular with people hooked on television. Collect the ones you feel will help you most. They will add to your dog smarts and may save you an emergency trip to the veterinarian.

CRATES

Don't cringe at the idea of a crate; it will be the best friend

Your dog's crate will be your dog's best friend. (After you, of course!)

your dog has besides yourself. You'll need a dog crate that will accommodate your dog's adult size.

A NEW NAME

Seems obvious enough, but how do you start? Even if your dog already has a name, most shelters suggest you rename him to remove any association with his past, especially if he's been abused. Of course pick out a name you like, but it's best to make it short and pleasant-sounding. Make sure your dog will be able to differentiate between his own name and your spouse and children and from commands like "No," "Sit," and "Come." Then use his name with meals and food treats and other good-dog situations. He'll figure it out. Avoid using his name during corrections so he only makes pleasant associations.

Use your dog's name in good-dog situations, such as mealtime. Snoopy is sure to come running when his name is called.

Mugsy McDuff and Mr. Higgins

Mugsy McDuff and Mr. Higgins were adopted from the Quincy Humane Society by Jean Mitchell. Mugsy, a schnauzer mix, insists on being in Jean's lap or under the covers in Jean's bed. Mr. Higgins was about 10 months old when he was found wandering loose in a river fishing camp. A laid-back southern gentleman, Mr. Higgins picks flowers for Jean every summer, leaving her with the only garden composed entirely of stalks. He helps her groom little kittens and teaches her other foster pups how to be dogs.

"Some mornings," Jean says, "lying in bed with the lump under the covers (Mugsy) and the bed hog (Mr. Higgins) across the bottom of the bed, I wonder at how blessed I am to have two such fine dogs."

"Mugsy McDuff "
& "Mr. Higgins"

"Jack"

Jack

J ack originally showed up as a stray at Claudette Ingram's home by jumping her fence to get *into* her yard. Jack's original owner gave him away because he wasn't mean enough, and his second owner had turned him loose and didn't want him back. When Claudette tried to help get Jack adopted, she became so emotionally involved with the dog that she adopted him herself! "There's not a mean bone in Jack's body," Claudette says proudly!

Dogproofing

YOUR HOUSE

Once you have your dog supplies laid in, it's time to examine your house and property. Do a room-by-room house check to make sure your home is safe for your new dog (and vice-versa). This is especially urgent if you're bringing home a puppy. Some hazards are more dangerous and may be fatal for a pup. You also want to eliminate anything that might create problems or tempta-

Dogs love to chew on things, so keep all electrical appliance cords safely hidden and unplugged when not in use.

tions in order to promote the most positive environment for your new dog by avoiding unnecessary or frivolous corrections.

1. Fasten all electrical cords to baseboards or move them out of reach. Electrical burns can range from serious to fatal.

2. Keep all medications, cleaning agents and similar materials out of open areas and locked up where your dog can't reach them. A curious dog or determined puppy can chew the lid off even a heavy bottle of toxic cleanser.

3. Never use pesticides or roach and rodent sprays or poisons in any area accessible to your dog. Don't assume the dog won't find it...he'll surprise you by doing what you least expect.

4. Always keep the lid down on the toilet and avoid the use of bowl cleaners in case your dog gets into the water despite your best efforts. It seems all dogs are born with a radar that attracts them to a toilet bowl.

5. Never throw chicken or turkey bones in your usual garbage container, and keep the trash secured where your dog can't dig after other tempting garbage that could choke or harm him.

6. Antifreeze will kill your dog. Animals are attracted to its sweet taste and even a few drops can kill an average-size dog. Clean up all spills immediately and keep containers locked or well secured.

7. Check your house and yard for plants that might be toxic to your dog and place all house plants out of a puppy's reach. You can obtain a list of dangerous plants from your veterinarian or local library. Some common house and yard plants can make your dog extremely ill or can be fatal if ingested.

9. Remove cigarettes and cigarette butts from ashtrays and other dog-convenient places. Ingested cigarettes can lead to nicotine poisoning.

10. At Christmas, keep all decorations out of your dog's reach. Puppies especially can dispose of a dangling ornament in the blink of an eye. Chocolate is

Holidays are an exciting time, but they can be dangerous for your dog. Keep Christmas decorations out of your dog's reach.

8. Weed killers and other herbicides are toxic to your dog as well as to your children. Some have residual effects for up to several days. Read the bag carefully. If you use a lawn service, have a serious discussion with your yard man. Many dog owners prefer to live with a few weeds rather than risk their dog's long-term health.

also highly toxic to dogs, as it contains a chemical called theobromine they are unable to metabolize. A 12-ounce bag of chocolate chips can kill a small dog; two bags would put a larger dog at serious risk. The danger is proportionate to the dog's weight. Hide those chocolate Santas and other chocolate treats.

"Play it again, Sam." Kids and canines make natural harmony together.

11. Consult your veterinarian before using any flea control products, especially on puppies under 16 weeks of age. Many are toxic to young dogs, and combining certain products can cause a toxic, even fatal reaction in dogs of any age.

12. Conduct a thorough check of your fencing or dog run/kennel to be sure there are no holes or weak areas your new dog could slip through.

13. Check all windows and screens for any that are loose and would allow a dog or puppy to fall through. Every year the Humane Society of the United States reports on dogs, cats and puppies who fall out of windows that were unsecured (or unsupervised!) and were injured or killed.

Everything you do to dogproof your home will not only make it safer for your dog, but will eliminate the possibility of "No-No's" or situations where you must correct the dog. The more positive the environment, the more successfully your dog will become a well behaved member of your family.

DOGPROOF THE KIDS

Did you know you need to dogproof your children at the same time you dogproof your house? One sad statistic tells us that many pets are surrendered to shelters because of problems between the animal and a child or children. Child psychologists now realize that very young children do not have a natural affinity for animals; rather they are unfeeling because they have not yet developed feelings of empathy or compassion and don't fully understand, so they are often cruel in their attitude toward a pet.

Teach your children—and their friends—that this dog or puppy is a living creature who is a friend

Children must be taught how to be gentle and properly handle their dogs. This toddler gives his Toy Poodle a great big hug.

and companion, not a toy to sit on or drag about. Show them how to be gentle and properly handle the dog. Never leave young children alone with a puppy or adult dog; a playful nip is painful and can easily break the skin, leaving the child fearful and resentful of the animal. Conversely, even innocent child's play can result in serious injury to a puppy or small dog.

Teach older children the correct way to hold a puppy or small dog, with a firm grip under the chest and stomach so the pup can't wiggle and fall. Never allow them to carry the dog around; he can easily injure himself in even a short fall.

Teach your children to respect a dog's needs and privacy. They

Kids and dogs are twice the fun...but they are also twice the work!

This young girl is helping her dog choose a Nylabone® toy to satisfy his chewing needs.

must allow him time and space for naps and meals and time-out. Emphasize that puppies and dogs need down time just like children do. Instruct them not to take the dog's food or disturb him when he's eating or sleeping; that's how dog bites happen.

Explain to your children that these rules apply to all dogs, not just your own. Tell them that all dogs are not friendly like theirs, that some may bite. Teach them never to approach a strange dog and to always ask permission from the owner before they pet a dog. Show them how to approach a dog to pet it: from the front with an outstretched hand for the dog to sniff first. Urge them to avoid any dog who growls or snarls or runs away.

Don't expect your children to be the primary caretakers of your dog. Sure they need to learn responsibility, but the dog's welfare is too important to be placed in the hands of kids who will be just that—kids. Let your child share in caring for the dog, but an adult member of the household should be fully responsible for the animal.

Infants and Toddlers

If your child is under three years old, you should think twice about getting a dog, especially a puppy. Kids and dogs might be twice the fun, but they are also double the work. Sure it's great for kids to grow up with a dog, but kids under three years of age don't understand animals. Both require your full-time attention, and when it comes to prioritizing, the dog will always come in second. And because neither dog nor child yet understands dog or kid rules, almost everything will be a "No-No," which creates a negative environment for both of them. In the event of a dog bite, or even a playful nip, the dog will always be the victim. It's best to wait until the child is older and able to follow instructions about living with a dog. Many breeders won't even sell a pup to families with children under five years old; it's in their dog's best interest.

Meanwhile, expose your youngsters to sweet-tempered dogs who live with friends or other family members, perhaps offer to dog-sit occasionally so your child will gradually learn how to treat an animal until such time when they can have a dog for their own best friend.

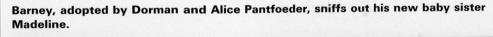

Barney, adopted by Dorman and Alice Pantfoeder, sniffs out his new baby sister Madeline.

Welcome Home

Make every effort to pick up your dog over a long weekend, vacation days or other periods when you'll have two or more days to spend with him. That will help minimize the risk of separation anxiety when you do leave him alone. It goes without saying to never bring a dog home at Christmas or other hectic holidays.

At the shelter or rescue home, allow time to learn every shred of information about your dog, background or family history, if you haven't already done so.

Review health matters and get the paperwork on his vaccinations. Find out what kind of food he's eating. If you plan to feed something else, it's wise to mix the two foods together and gradually increase the amount of the new ration to prevent intestinal upset from a new dog food. (Who needs diarrhea on his first day home?)

Bring your new collar, leash and ID tags; don't rely on whatever the dog might have. The leash is vital, since the dog may object to going with you. Bring a

Many shelters and humane societies display bulletin boards that boast happy "tails" of successful adoptions.

Peaches, a Greyhound, raced in Mobile, Alabama before she came to live with Cindy Cash. "She has, through me, given life to so many more," Cindy says.

companion or another family member to collect the dog. He may be afraid of cars or resist entering your vehicle, and you'll need a helper to comfort him during the trip home. Leave the kids at home. Changing environments is very stressful for a dog and fewer distractions will minimize the stress. Moreover, if the dog behaves badly, it will only create a negative impression that could leave a permanent imprint on your children.

PATIENCE AND UNDERSTANDING

When you're stocking up your dog essentials, be sure to lay in a generous supply of patience and understanding—you'll probably need both during your dog's first weeks at home. Of course you're a good guy and plan to love this dog forever, but he doesn't know that yet. He may act frightened or shy, in fact, he probably will. He might misbehave or try to run away. He's naturally insecure about his new surroundings.

A PEACEFUL WELCOME

Make the dog's homecoming as peaceful and uneventful as possible, no welcome home celebrations with relatives or your children's friends. Children especially should not smother the dog with too much attention and excitement. This may be his second or third home so he needs quiet time to adjust to his new

Maureen...who can resist bringing a sweet Beagle face into their home?

space and learn to trust his new human family.

Walk the dog on a leash around your yard and through allowable areas of the house so he can sniff and investigate every nook and corner. Show him his water supply and eating area if it's separate from his water bowl. Don't assume the dog will automatically know his dog things. Introduce him to his crate and/or sleeping area. The crate should be kept in a quiet place, but not removed from family activity so the dog won't feel isolated from the family.

LEARNING THE NEW ROPES

For the first day or two, set your cooking timer for 60 minutes and every hour or so take him to the same place in the yard where he can relieve himself. Even if he's house trained, the stress of a new environment could set his habits back. Your passwords are still praise, patience and persistence. Puppies, of course, require the entire gamut of training procedures, since they have no history to draw on. Read that book you bought on puppy training. Check out another book or two on obedience training if your new dog is an adult or older puppy.

These first days are important in establishing your role as your dog's pack leader. He needs to learn that you're in charge or he'll gladly assume that chore himself. He also needs to feel wanted and loved. That means quality time, constant supervision and play time, and confinement when you

A walk, on a leash, around your home and yard is a great way to accustom dogs to a new home. Jock and Toto tip toe through the tulips.

Encourage constructive chewing by offering your dog a safe chew toy. Gumabones® are great for young puppies due to their softer composition.

stimulate him. How exciting for you both!

Your children's new-dog rules should apply to everyone. Don't lavish heaps of attention on the dog and don't cave in if he's demanding. Leaders don't take orders, so offer him love and attention on your terms only (not when he nudges your elbow or whines to be petted some more—then he's giving the orders). Maintain a calm and quiet atmosphere until the dog settles into a comfortable routine.

Routine is important to his adjustment. Your daily activities, coming and going, should be consistent so the dog learns he can depend on you. A newly adopted dog is often very insecure in a new environment...can you blame him? He's been abandoned once, maybe more. It's your job to build his confidence and convince him that he—and you—are here to stay.

If your adoptee is a puppy, you can practice these leadership exercises by Drs. Line and Engle of the Hennepin County Animal Humane Society. It will help turn your puppy into a confident, friendly, eager-to-lease adult. Many of these exercises will work with adult dogs as well.

can't be with him. No free time for a while; he doesn't know the rules and could easily misbehave because he doesn't know better.

He also needs to be socialized like any other new member of the family. At home for the first week or so, then out and about so he can become confident in his new world. In the house, keep him with you while you read or watch TV. Have him tag along during your normal household routine of cooking, laundry and other chores to maximize your time together. It's important to just be there.

Gradually expand your daily walks to include new places, sounds and smells...the neighborhood park, grocery store, other shops, a friend's back yard. Each new adventure will intrigue and

Leadership Exercises for Families and Puppies

Practice these leadership exercises as the situations occur throughout the day. They will help turn your puppy into a confident, friendly dog that is eager to please all members of the family—adults and children alike.

Do:	**Don't:**
Have your puppy sit and wait while you go through outside doors first.	Let your puppy run through the doorway ahead of you.
Have your puppy wait for her meal until after people have had their dinner.	Let your puppy eat before you or at the same time.
Teach your puppy to accept being touched while he eats.	Avoid disturbing your puppy while he's eating.
Gently move your puppy out of the way if she is lying in your path.	Step around your puppy or choose another route so she isn't disturbed.
Have your puppy obey a request like sit before receiving attention.	Pet your puppy whenever he comes to demand attention from you.
If your puppy stares at you, stare back until he looks away.	Break eye contact first if your puppy stares at you.
Pet your puppy with long, slow strokes starting at the top of head and continuing to the shoulders.	Pet your puppy with quick, short strokes across the head or face that get her excited.
Play games like fetch, with you in control of the toys at the end.	Play games like tug of war, where your puppy is likely to win.
Teach your puppy that hands are not appropriate chew toys.	Encourage your puppy to bite your hands by playing games with his mouth.
Practice touching and handling your puppy's feet, mouth, and ears.	Avoid touching your puppy's feet, mouth, and ears.
Practice the controlled down exercise and let your puppy up when she relaxes.	Put your puppy on his back, then let her escape or give up if she struggles.
Speak in a soft, high-pitched, praising voice so your puppy is eager to pay attention.	Speak in loud, low tones—a firm threatening voice so your puppy knows you mean business.

A SECOND DOG

If you have another family dog you must plan carefully for the introduction. Never bring a rescue or shelter dog into your home and let the two dogs introduce themselves. Your normally sweet dog may resent this new intruder and will have at it before you can catch your breath.

It's best to introduce the dogs on neutral ground, at a nearby park or isolated public area. Both dogs should be on leash, with one person to attend each dog. Be sure to maintain a loose leash, as tension on the leash may signal to each dog that the other is a threat and he could assume an aggressive posture. Allow both dogs to approach each other and sniff for about 10 to 15 seconds. Use verbal praise and happy talk when they show signs of normal curiosity. Then call them apart in a casual manner without pulling on the leash. If there were no signs of aggression, repeat the meeting for slightly longer. If the dogs play bow and tails wag, let them play together with leashes on for security, then take them for a walk together, both on lead. Repeat the on-leash play process in your back yard. Supervise the dogs' time together until a firm friendship is established... some take more time to bond than others. Feed them separately but at the same time (very often the subordinate dog will choose not to eat his food until the dominant dog is finished with his meal) and don't allow them to share toys

Ali enjoys her two adopted brothers, Duke and Bogart. Owners, Jim and Debbie Gardner.

until they prove reliable together. Be fair and equal with your attention so your original dog doesn't feel neglected or left out.

Both dogs will have to establish a pecking order between them, and some minor scuffling may ensue. Do not allow or at least minimize opportunities for dis-

Never risk a dog bite to break up a fight. Cold water from a hose or pitcher will sometimes end a battle, or you can shove a chair or other large object between the dogs. Always speak firmly during a scuffle so the dogs know it's not another dog who is entering the fray.

Dogs and cats usually work through their own introductions. Meuniere and Moon, a Labrador Retriever, get acquainted. Owner, Connie Howard.

putes to arise. Never allow them to escalate. Separate the animals calmly and without punishment. It's always better to deflect a fight with distractions or obedience commands. If serious or prolonged fighting occurs, contact your shelter or adoption coordinator for further advice.

THE FAMILY CAT

If you have a cat, don't force an introduction and don't restrain the cat. Just make sure it has an escape route when you bring your new dog home. They will usually work things out on their own terms.

Molly & Buster

Molly, a Chow mix, was Laurie and Tom Edmondson's first adopted shelter dog. When she first came home, Molly always laid with her back to every wall as if she needed to protect herself. Although friendly from the start, she was still a bit aloof and it seemed like she wasn't sure anyone would ever *really* love her. After a month of loving care, she finally felt like she was part of the family, right down to sleeping in the bedroom with Tom and Laurie.

Buster, Laurie's second shelter dog, was adopted because her son Jake wanted a dog to sleep in his room like Molly did with his parents. Molly was very assertive with Buster, and at their first meeting she pinned him alpha-dog style to explain that she was the boss. At first Buster acted "hang-dog" and respected her but now they're equal partners and best buddies. Buster is also crate-trained (Laurie calls it his "apartment.") and whenever he's in his crate, Molly always lies right beside it. "They were easy to train," Laurie said. "We just used common sense."

"Molly"

"Buster"

Benefits of a Crate and How to Use It

Use of a pet crate is the best way to give your dog a way to "get away from it all." It's also great for housebreaking as well as child-proofing. The crate is a critical key to the success of your new dog's adoption program.

Yes, you or other family members or friends may view the crate as cruel and inhumane, a jail or unholy place. Your dog doesn't see it that way.

From the dog's perspective, he now has a room of his own, a place where he feels safe and secure, a sanctuary, an indoor dog house if you will. A crate satisfies the natural "den" instinct that he inherited from his den-dwelling ancestors. From his perspective, it's not a cage he can't get out of—it's his very own territory where humans can't get in! And wouldn't you appreciate a place where he can't get into trouble rather than left to his other instincts that lead to shredding and chewing whatever isn't nailed down.

The crate then offers peace of mind for both you and your dog. You can leave your dog home alone knowing he is comfortable and protected, and so are your home and possessions. This also spares your dog the fear and confusion he'll endure when you come home and discover he chewed your sofa cushions or antique table legs while you were gone. Even if you don't scold, you'll still be upset and he'll sense it. That's what dogs are good at.

With crate use you can confine your dog when you have guests, children, or anyone else who might overly excite him or lead him to disruptive behavior. You also can travel safely with your dog. He's tucked into his own canine baby seat and can't jump in your lap, an obvious safety precaution for both of you when

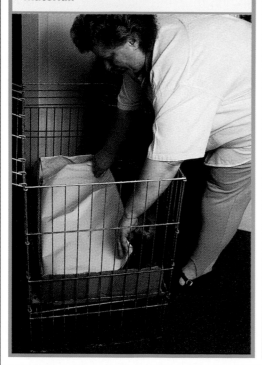

Make your dog's crate a cozy, comfortable retreat. Line it with a soft blanket or towel or other washable material.

you're motoring on the interstate at 65 m.p.h. Your crated dog will be welcome at motels, and even your grumpy maiden aunt can't complain if he's crated when you visit.

A crate's greatest value is in housebreaking your dog or puppy. It allows you to capitalize on a canine's natural instinct not to soil his den and to establish a regular routine for outdoor elimination. The crate will also prevent accidents at night and whenever he must be left alone. By now you have to believe the crate is actually a gilded cage!

While the crate will be your dog's favorite place to be, make sure you don't abuse it. Never place your dog in his crate in anger. Sure you can use it as

A crate is the safest way to travel with a dog—it is like a canine baby seat!

The crate can be your dog's favorite safe place; NEVER use it in anger.

"punishment," only he shouldn't know that.

A crate is never recommended for a dog who must be left alone for long periods of time. As a general rule, a dog shouldn't be crated for more than four or five hours at a time, puppies never more than three. Leave the radio on during your absence; the sound of music and a human voice will soothe him while you're gone.

If you can't tend your dog for long periods of time, enlist the aid of a neighbor or friend who can come over to let the dog out to relieve himself and stretch his legs. If no such person is available, consider using a doggie day care on those extra-long days.

SELECTING A CRATE

There are two types of crates available: wire mesh and the fiberglass or plastic airline crate. Either one is fine. The airline crate is more den-like, while advocates of wire mesh crates feel they allow better ventilation and make the dog feel less isolated. Your dog won't care. He'll adapt to whatever you decide on. If you use a wire crate, you can cover it with an old sheet or large towel to enhance the den-like environment when it's time to sleep.

The crate should be large enough for an adult dog to lie down without being cramped and sit up without hitting his head. That may be tough to predict if you have a mixed breed pup who could grow beyond your expectations. You'll just have to take your best guess. Your vet or shelter worker should be able to suggest the proper size. It's best to have the crate set up when you bring your new dog home so you can begin crate conditioning right away.

CRATE CONDITIONING

While your dog will feel secure when he's crated, you still want him to feel like he's part of the family unit. Place the crate in a

Two types of crates: the fiberglass crates are more den-like, while the metal crates allow better air circulation.

"people" area of the house, a corner of the family room or kitchen, so he won't be totally isolated from you. It may not be the most attractive piece of furniture in the room, but it does come in handy as an extra table top.

At night move the crate into your bedroom so your dog won't feel left alone again. Sleeping in his crate next to your bed will also continue the bonding process through the night. A puppy especially needs to know you're close by even when he's snoozing. You'll also be able to hear him stir or whimper if he has to go out, which will aid in housebreaking. Puppies rarely "hold it" through the night, and even adult dogs in a new and strange environment may need to relieve themselves due to stress or anxiety.

It's never a good idea to allow your dog to sleep with you (at least not in the beginning!). To a dog (and lesser pack member) on your bed means equal, and will seriously diminish your position in the leader role. For people who like a furry critter in their bed, wait until the dog is thoroughly trained and full of respect for your authority. Make bed-sharing a privilege gained only by permission from Number One. And he must also learn the "Off" command. If he refuses to leave when asked, won't share his bed space or shows even a small sign of dominance like a curled lip or muted growl, the bed becomes off limits pronto. Ditto for your children's beds.

Make the crate a cozy place; toss in a couple of chew toys, such as Nylabones® or Gumabones®, plus an old towel or blanket so he has something comfy to curl up on. Nothing of value in case he shreds it (don't replace it if he does), and something you can wash if he soils it. An article of clothing like an old bathrobe or sweatshirt with your scent on it sometimes works to comfort the dog. You may have to

Purchase the right size crate. It should be big enough for an adult dog to sit and stand comfortably.

experiment with a crate rug or towel to see what works. Every dog is different.

Now teach your dog to accept his new den by tossing a bit of a food treat into the crate while he's watching. Leave the food in the crate until he takes it, then praise him when he does. Some dogs will dash right in, while others are more skeptical and have to mus-

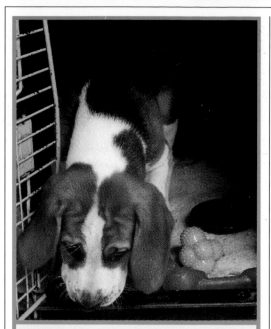

Toss a few of your pup's favorite Nylabones® in his crate to keep him occupied.

ter up their courage to investigate. You can also feed the first few meals in the crate with the crate door open to create a pleasant association. Leave those chew toys in the crate so he can amuse himself when he's crated and awake. Use a kennel command such as "Kennel" or "Crate" when the dog goes in. Remember that important dog rule about word association.

After he's been going in and out comfortably, gradually close the door and leave it closed for just a minute or two, then release him. No big fanfare coming out, make it a non-event. No treats or big hugs so he won't be anxious to come out for those rewards. His reward is simply being once again with you.

Don't allow him to bark while crated. Whether he's protesting confinement or just singing along with Sinatra, he must learn to be quiet in his den. If he barks persistently (and you know it's not a potty call) smack the top of the crate with your hand or a book and order "Quiet!" When he shuts up, tell him "Good Dog." If the crate is covered with a sheet or blanket when you swat it, he'll think his barking caused a piece of the sky to fall. Never release him from his crate when he's noisy or he'll think barking got him out. It's that association thing again.

Even if things don't go smoothly at first, don't weaken and don't worry. You're doing your dog a favor by preventing mischief when he's left alone, so it's worth the effort. Almost every dog will accept crating; it's just a matter of time.

Once he's staying in the closed crate, extend the period of time he spends in there; it shouldn't take more than a day or three to accomplish this. Now you can move ahead to establish a solid housebreaking routine.

CRATES AND HOUSEBREAKING

In the beginning take your dog out every hour or two until he gets used to the idea of going out. Use the same door each time, and until he's reliable, confine your dog to the area of the house nearest the door he's supposed to use. (If he's at the other end of the house and has to relieve himself, he won't know where the exit is.) Baby gates make a good containment system. Then gradually introduce him to other allowable areas of his new home, one room at a time so all these strange surroundings won't overwhelm him. It's less stressful for a dog of any age to explore new places on a limited basis, and it won't upset the housebreaking apple cart.

Take him to the same place outside every time and praise him like a hero for doing his job. Use key words, such as "Get busy" or "Hurry up," so he'll learn what these little trips outside are all about. When he goes, repeat the key word along with the praise, "Good boy, get busy, good boy, get busy." He'll soon figure it out. Some dogs learn to use the same place for elimination, and others end up using the entire yard. You won't care, as long as he goes outdoors.

Even if you have a fenced back-yard, you still have to accompany a puppy or adult dog on every bathroom outing, rain or snow, midnight or 3 a.m., so you can be sure he's done his business *and* so you can lay on the praise. Remember those key words...and the three "Ps."

During the housebreaking process, puppies will need to be crated more than an adult dog because they have so little blad-der control and they haven't learned to recognize that "gotta go" feeling in advance. A pup should be crated at night, during naps, and whenever you're not able to watch him. If puppy falls asleep at your feet, just pick him up and place him in his crate to finish his nap. Be sure to close the door. Otherwise guess what? He'll probably wake up, toddle out of his den to piddle, then run over to you to say hello. Behind closed doors, he'll whine or yip when he wakes up. And puppies *always* have to go when they wake up!

Take puppy out to relieve him-self every time he leaves his crate. Puppies also need to eliminate when they first wake up in the morning, after naps and play time, within a short period after eating and before going to bed at night.

Be observant and monitor your dog or puppy's signals when he has to go out: sniffing the floor, starting to squat, circling at the door, maybe just walking to the door with a quick glance, then

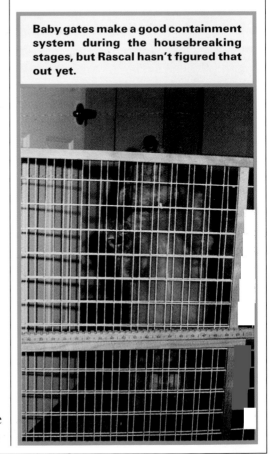

Baby gates make a good containment system during the housebreaking stages, but Rascal hasn't figured that out yet.

back to you. Each dog develops his own message system, and if you're not there in seconds, it will be puddle-time. It's up to you to make sure he's as successful as possible to build good habits you both can live with.

When you're mopping up those messes, be sure to thoroughly disinfect and deodorize the soiled areas. His nose will know, and your dog will return to those spots if they retain his smell. After blotting and cleaning with a good commercial cleaner, saturate the spot with a spray of 50/50 vinegar water. Cover with a folded towel and place a book over the towel for 24 hours. Then think up a clever excuse for your neighbors about why you have books all over the living room rug.

More about those little accidents (accidents defined as times you don't see the dog do it)…when they happen, just bite the bullet and resolve to be more watchful. Never discipline your dog or puppy for an accident you discover after the fact. Dogs only understand this moment in time and will not connect a correction with a past deed. Punishing him even seconds later will only create a fearful dog—you have to catch him in the act. Then use a firm "No!" or "Aaahh, aaahh!" and whisk him outside. Occasionally the shock of your sudden reprimand may even cause the dog to stop piddling and he'll finish the job outside. **NEVER** strike a dog with your hand or a newspaper or rub his

Take your puppy to the same place outside to relieve himself every time and praise him lavishly for doing his job.

It is the owner's responsibility to make sure her dog is successfully housetrained and learns good habits that they both can live with.

nose in his mess. Such tactics are extreme and will only cause fear and confusion in the dog and further complicate the housebreaking process.

There are many books available today that specifically address issues such as housebreaking and teaching house manners. Reading one or two of them will add to your arsenal of dog knowledge, make you a better and more responsible dog owner and produce a better dog.

Your Dog's New Life

VISIT THE VETERINARIAN

Your dog's first venture into his new world should be to his veterinarian. Try to make his vet visit pleasant so he won't associate the car with a possibly stressful examination in a strange environment.

Find a vet you can trust and feel comfortable with. Friends or neighbors who have dogs are good referral sources. A good relationship with your vet will be good for both you and your dog.

Bring along the dog's health records if you have them and a stool sample on this first visit.

You should take your dog to the veterinarian immediately following his adoption and maintain regular veterinary check-ups throughout his life.

Ask lots of questions about dog care in general. How much should he eat, how often should he be bathed, how do I trim his nails, clean his ears. Take your time, ask for demonstrations and take notes. Also ask about heartworm medication. Your veterinarian will complete or plan the dog's vaccination schedule if needed. He also will explain you must visit at least once a year to update your dog's shots and check for heartworm and other internal parasites.

Obtain a canine first aid guide so you can recognize emergency situations and be prepared to handle them. (Yes, they do happen in all dog families!) It's much easier—and healthier—to prevent emergency situations from happening than it is to deal with them. This is also a good time to start a dog diary to keep your dog's health record current and health care information handy. (Now when are those shots due again???)

FEEDING AND NUTRITION

Be sure to discuss dog food with your veterinarian. Most vets recommend a quality dry kibble food appropriate for each dog's age and activity level. Avoid generic and store brands as they usually are made with inferior products and will not provide complete or adequate nutrition.

Establish a meal routine and feed at the same time once or

twice a day. A regular feeding schedule is especially important for your adopted dog who needs these constants in his life to feel secure again. Puppies should eat three times daily until four or five months of age, then switch to twice a day. Don't free-feed adults or puppies and never leave the food out for the dog to eat at his whimsy. It plays havoc with elimination habits and housebreaking. A regular feeding schedule supports housebreaking and helps prevent obesity.

Always offer the food in the same place and leave it out for about 20 minutes. If the dog doesn't eat or finish it, remove the bowl and don't add the unfinished portion to the next meal—offer the same amount each time.

Don't worry if he's off his feed his first day or two at home. Dogs are less apt to starve themselves than they are to overeat and get too fat. Never feed your dog table scraps, even if he refuses to eat his own food. If your dog is a poor eater, try a different (not cheaper) dry food or sprinkle a bit of garlic

Feed your dog a dry kibble food appropriate for his age and activity level.

or onion powder over the food—most dogs love it! You can also try mixing a small amount of canned food with the dry. Canned food is less nutritious and contains approximately 75 percent water, but most dogs love the flavor and will gobble their dry food if it's enhanced with a canned product.

Just like carrots, Carrot Bones® are rich in fiber, carbohydrates, and Vitamin A. These durable chews contain no plastics or artificial ingredients of any kind. They can be served as is, in a bone-hard form, or microwaved to a biscuit consistency.

A note of caution: No vitamins or supplements for puppies. Puppy food is especially balanced for proper growth and adding your own goodies could affect growth patterns. Most veterinary nutritionists advise a quality puppy food only.

Allow your dog access to water at all times. For dogs of all ages, avoid heavy exercise an hour before and two hours after feeding.

EXERCISE

Speaking of exercise...regular exercise is as important as a good diet for your dog. Not only will it help prevent obesity (in your dog and you!), it will keep your dog physically stimulated and satisfied and less apt to venture into Seek and Destroy missions around the house. The amount of exercise depends on the size, breed and temperament of the dog, but as a rule, a half-hour

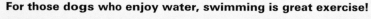

For those dogs who enjoy water, swimming is great exercise!

When bathing your dog, use a good quality dog shampoo that won't strip the oils from his coat.

GROOMING AND BATHING

Your dog also needs to be kept clean and groomed. Clean is a given, according to whatever bathing regimen your veterinarian recommends. Use a quality dog shampoo (people shampoo is too harsh) that won't strip the natural oils from his coat.

Grooming is the hands-on part your dog will love the most. Not only will frequent (at least twice a week) brushing keep your dog handsome and presentable, it will become part of the bonding process, stroking the dog as you comb and brush, with your dog responding to your touch. What better way for both of you to relax and enjoy each other's company?

Agility games are fun for both dog and owner. This Springer mix sails through the tire jump.

walk twice a day will keep the average dog in decent shape. High-energy dogs might need additional activity, like fetch games with a Frisbee. Swimming is great all-around exercise if you have a pond nearby and a dog who thinks he's a fish (and many do!).

Agility games and exercises are also great energy expenders and fun for the owner as well as the dog. Local kennel clubs and dog training clubs may offer agility classes or access to agility equipment. Agility has grown into a major dog sport and entertainment form. Try it. You'll both love it!

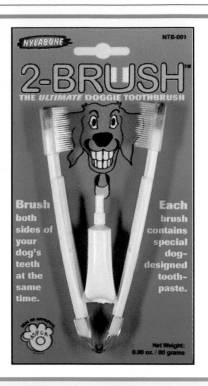

2-Brush® is made with two toothbrushes to clean both sides of your dog's teeth at the same time. Each brush contains a toothpaste reservoir designed to apply the toothpaste, which is specially formulated for dogs, directly into the brush.

DENTAL CARE

To keep your dog's smile white and shining, keep him supplied with dental chew toys like sterile marrow bones, Nylabones® and Nylafloss®. Feeding dry food, POPpups®, Carrot Bones®, or Roar-Hide® also helps keep plaque and tartar to a minimum. Clean his teeth once a week with a gauze pad dipped in baking soda or doggie toothpaste. (People toothpaste will make him sick.) If you're hesitant or squeamish, your veterinarian can show you how.

TEACHING AND TRAINING

Continuing up the dog ladder, your well-fed, exercised and well-groomed dog has to be well-trained or he won't be fit to live with. Loving him is not enough to produce proper canine behavior...but you already knew that!

Refer back to word association and positive reinforcement. That's the basis of all dog training, whether puppy or adult. Positive reinforcement makes desirable behaviors pleasurable for the dog so he will want to repeat the behavior. He does what you ask, you praise him or offer a food reward, he remembers.

Negative associations work the same way. Your dog is naughty (fill in the blank: jumps on the furniture, steals food off the counter, nips your fingers...the list is endless...), something unpleasant happens (a correction appropriate to the naughty behavior: a shaker can falls out of nowhere, a squirt of vinegar or lemon juice from a spray bottle, a muzzle squeeze or collar shake...) and he'll remember and develop some respect. That's avoidance training.

However, if he gets into mischief (mischief defined as something you don't want him to do only he doesn't know that yet) and he succeeds because nothing unpleasant occurs, that's also reinforcement and guess what...he'll do it again! What better reason to watch him every minute or put him in his den if you can't.

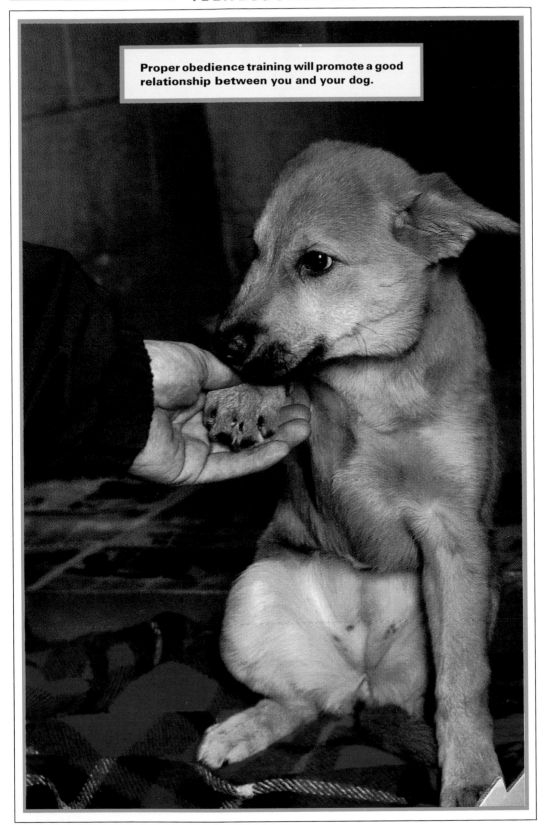

Proper obedience training will promote a good relationship between you and your dog.

Duke

Jim Gardner and his son, Erik, visited the local SPCA several times looking for "just the right dog" as a companion for their Labrador Retriever, Ali. After several visits, their patience was rewarded when they discovered a huge, statuesque black Labrador. The dog was unusually and elegantly responsive and extended his great black paws in a gentle introduction. Jim and Erik visited the dog six times before bringing the entire family to join him on his journey to his new home. He became "Duke," pride of the Gardner family, best friend to Ali, and to all others, a haunting black dog who stands tall amidst his canine peers.

"Duke"

"Wave"

Wave

Wave was two years old when the Gilbert family rescued her from her second owner. The huge brown Chesapeake Bay Retriever had been seriously neglected and was infested with parasites and suffered from liver and kidney damage. Yet her exuberance and lively attitude instantly captured the Gilberts' hearts. Wave spent her first months in and out of the hospital struggling to regain her health. Although her recovery would require medication and a special diet that would last throughout her life, she became like a third child to parents Pete and Diane, a loyal playmate and friend to their daughters Amy and Lauren, and a neighborhood favorite for 11 years.

Dog Training 101: Some Basic Principles

A dog's first lesson must be that you're the one in charge. All dogs learn by repetition.

You give a command once—you mean what you say.

Never give a command you can't reinforce or follow through.

Use short, crisp commands. "Quiet," "Down," "Easy." (Don't muck it up with lots of conversation, "Ginger, I told you to Sit and I mean it, for heaven's sake! SIT, will you please SIT!") Teach lessons with rewards and/or displeasure.

Put some oomph into your voice. If you say "No, no," but your voice says "Please," your dog probably won't believe you or obey.

Firm does not mean nasty or angry.

Use a high-pitched happy voice during training sessions.

No hitting or yelling allowed. It could injure the dog and will set back his training as well as his attitude about the person he's trying to please (you).

Never call your dog to you to discipline him.

Be patient. Some dogs learn quickly, others take more time.

Be consistent. If you allow a behavior today (sitting on the sofa with you) but not tomorrow (when

These dogs practice "Down" with distractions during training class. Formal obedience classes are a great way to socialize your dog.

your sister visits), how will your dog ever know what you expect of him? The rules apply all the time.

Be positive. Believe your dog is smart and will learn his lessons well. He will sense your trust...that's what dogs do best.

BASIC OBEDIENCE COMMANDS EVERY GOOD DOG SHOULD KNOW

Of course you and your dog plan to attend a weekly obedience class to learn the best way to communicate with each other. It will be your night out together plus provide you with an incentive to work with your dog between classes so you'll be the best team there (and won't look foolish because you didn't practice!)

But don't wait for a training class to start teaching your dog good manners. Certain command words must become part of your dog's vocabulary if you're to live in peace and harmony together. Start your training in a quiet familiar place without distractions. As the dog becomes more proficient, move your sessions to different places like your driveway or a neighbor's yard (if you have good neighbors). Gradually add outside distractions during his session. Parks, mall areas and grocery store parking lots are typical places to advance to. A dog who sits in his own living room but not at the beach or park is not a trained or well-behaved dog.

Make training sessions short, five or ten minutes, shorter lessons for a puppy. Work on one command at a time and repeat each command eight or ten times

per session. Don't overdo it or you'll bore the dog. You can use a combination of food treats, verbal and hands-on praise and physical coercion to teach the meaning of each command. What works best with one dog won't motivate another.

The Release Word

Devise a release word so your dog will know when the training

The author practices retriever training with a group of Goldens.

session ends or when you want him to take a break in between. "Break" or "Free" are in fact the words preferred. "Okay" is too common in our daily conversation and could confuse the dog. Don't use the dog's name when giving "Sit" and "Down" (stationary) commands. Do use his name in combination with moving commands such as "Let's Go" and "Come."

Start each workout with a leash and training collar on your dog. It's also helpful to exercise your dog a bit before you train. It will take the edge off his energy and boost his attention level.

Sit

Food training works wonders with a pup and many adult dogs learn more easily with food. Use tiny bits of puppy biscuit or slices of hot dog cut in half. Stand in front of the dog, hold the treat just above his nose and move it slightly backwards over the top of his head. Not too high or he'll stand on his rear feet to reach it. He should tilt backwards for the

Start each training session with a leash and training collar.

Soft Coated Wheaten Terrier at "Down." Hand signals help reinforce verbal commands.

food with his rear sliding toward the floor. Say the command once as you maneuver the food. As soon as the dog's rump hits the floor, praise him, "Good dog, Sit!" and give the treat. If he resists putting his rump down, you may have to help him out and push it down with your other hand. When you dispense the food, use the other hand to scratch his ear as part of the hands-on praise. Eventually and intermittently, remove the food and praise with just your voice and hands. You may have to practice to find the right angle for the food. Do at least eight to ten repetitions with the food.

If you can't manipulate your dog with food, use the tried-and-true method of teaching "Sit." Place the dog at your left side, hold the leash in your right hand with most of the slack curled in your hand. Tell the dog to "Sit," once only, pull up with the leash to move his upper body backwards and push his rump down with your left hand. As above, the instant his rear end hits the floor, praise him with a "Good boy, Sit!" Use happy conversation to let him know how good he is, "What a wonderful boy you are! Good dog!"

Down

Puppies learn everything best with food! When teaching "Down," don't use a "Sit" word first. Simply hold the bit of food to the dog's nose, tell him "Down," once, and lower the treat to the floor, pushing backwards toward the dog's front feet. Keep pushing the food backwards at floor level, forcing the dog to lower his body to the floor. The moment all four legs are down, tell him "Good dog,

Training equipment: leashes, collars, treats, dumbbell, and a soft ball. Not pictured: a positive attitude!

Be sure you praise while the dog is still sitting so he doesn't confuse praise with releasing from the "Sit" position. Puppies will take longer to master each command. Even though they're usually eager students, there's a whole world full of goodies to investigate!

Down" and give the food. Rub his ears with your free hand at the same time. Once the dog has mastered "Down" and "Sit," wait just a bit longer each time to give the food so he learns not to break position. That's the beginning of the "Stay" command.

Use "Off" instead of "Down" when training your dog to stay off furniture.

Off

As in get off the furniture or with jumping. Using "Off" instead of "Down" is less confusing to the dog.

Wait and Stay

Once your dog responds well to "Sit" and "Down," add the "Stay" command. Gradually increase the time in ten-second increments as well as your distance from the dog. "Wait" sends a different message to the dog. Use "Wait" when going in and out the door, instructing your dog that you go first like all leaders do. "Sit-Wait" means "in a minute" if he's prancing for his food dish. A smart dog (and yours is that) will learn the difference quickly. Your obedience class and a good book on obedi-ence training will explain the details of these exercises.

Give or Leave It

Use this command word and his name when removing forbidden objects from your dog's mouth. If he won't release it willingly, squeeze his muzzle by pressing his flews (lips) against his teeth and gums while saying "Give" and remove the object with your other hand. Praise him when he releases it, whether by force or otherwise. Give him a tidbit in return. You must be able to remove food or other objects from your dog's mouth. A dog who guards his food bowl or his toys is a potential biter and must learn it is you who giveth and you who taketh away. If this becomes a problem, consult a professional trainer to work it out.

Walking on a Leash

Before your dog will do this nicely, he has to be comfortable with the leash. Most dogs learn to love their leash because they know it means "Out." But it's not uncommon at first for a dog to object violently and tug and pull in every direction except the right one. If you didn't let him drag the leash around the house, now's the time to start. Attach the leash to his buckle collar for a couple hours each day for two or three days.

When you start your walk together, tell your dog "Let's go," in a happy voice. Don't use the word "Heel" because Heel is actu-ally a position, the place next to your left leg during a walk. All you need to accomplish at first is that he walk along with you within two or three feet without pulling on the leash. Walk around your yard or driveway, move ahead briskly and chat with him as you go, "O-kay, good boy!" This is a fun time and eventually you're going to tour the neighborhood together.

Keep the leash loose with a little slack in it. When he moves too far ahead, tell him "Easy," with a quick tug or pop on the leash to bring him back to you. If he lags or dawdles, repeat "Let's go," and pop him forward. Walk straight ahead at first, turning in very wide circles that don't require a hard turn. Once in a while turn around and walk in the opposite direction, telling him "Let's go!" with a tug on the leash, then "Good boy!" when he's alongside you again. Be sure to praise him when he looks at you or when he follows each maneuver. No praise unless he's where he should be, but don't scold him if he's not. Let the leash make the correction while your voice tells him what fun this is.

If he's doing well, walk for a minute or two, then stop with a "Break" command and give him a good hug. Repeat the process for three or four times. He won't really understand this walking business until he's got the hang of it. If he fights or struggles with the leash, limit walking to 10 or 12 successful paces, then take a "Good Dog!" break. Increase the walking distance as your dog improves. Once he's walking well you can practice in different places like you did with Sit and Down.

Come

Coming to you should be the happiest thing your dog ever does. Keep that thought uppermost whenever you tell your dog to "Come."

You can start teaching "Come" as a separate command while teaching the ones we've just discussed. Attach a 10- or 12-foot lead or lightweight long line to his collar. Hold the other end and call him to you using his name and "Come." If he doesn't come imme-diately, tug and reel him in to you as you turn and run backwards so he thinks it's a game. Face the dog when he reaches you, tell him he's fabulous and give him a treat along with a hug. Acting like a

When practicing "Heel," your dog should be positioned next to your left leg, without pulling forward or lagging behind.

silly fool (you) will enhance the game. (Repeat—this is important—coming to mom or dad should always be his favorite thing to do.)

As with earlier commands, say "Come" only once so he doesn't think that it's a three or four word command. Start by calling your dog only when you're sure he will respond. It's important to make every call a big success. Be creative and set up situations so you're sure your pal will come.

Gradually work at greater distances using a longer line of 20 to 30 feet. Now wait until the dog is distracted, call his name with the command and a tug on the rope if he doesn't come at once. Continue with intermittent food rewards until he's totally reliable. You never eliminate the verbal and hands-on praise, that's your lifelong gift to him.

Until your dog is totally reliable coming when he's called, just keep that 20-foot line on him whenever he's outdoors. The dog won't mind a bit and you'll have that all-important control you need. It's not uncommon for puppies to wear a long line until they're one year old.

The cardinal rule of "Come" is never (that's spelled N-E-V-E-R)

The "Come" command is the most important command your dog will learn; it could someday save his life.

Some people teach the hand signal for "Come" along with the verbal command.

discipline or scold a dog when he comes to you. That's the quickest way to turn "Come" into "Go Away Fast." The dog will associate coming to you with the punishment, not with running away, sniffing about or whatever he did (or you thought he did) wrong. Then guess what? He won't want to come anymore and can you blame him? You also shouldn't call your dog to come for anything he might find unpleasant like baths or giving medication. Go and get him instead.

Remember to say it only once. If he doesn't come after a single command, don't repeat the command. Instead go to him, hook up his leash, grit your teeth and try again. Some behaviors take more time to instill and this one is important; it could save his life.

Problem Behaviors

SEPARATION ANXIETY

Separation anxiety is caused when the dog is isolated from his owner or person he loves. It can also occur even if the dog thinks you might be leaving. He doesn't understand that you'll return and he gets anxious, stressed and fearful. It's no surprise then that separation anxiety is common among shelter dogs who think they're being abandoned once again. Typical reactions, ranging from mild to severe, include excessive barking, destructiveness and inappropriate elimination.

Dr. Karen Overall at the Department of Clinical Studies, School of Veterinary Medicine, University of Pennsylvania, found that canine attention-seeking behavior was a forerunner or milder version of separation anxiety. An emotionally needy dog that nudges you, sits on your foot or obsessively follows you around may anticipate or "experience" your absence, even when you're there with him. She suggests curbing such dependence by spending time with your dog in daily activities such as running, brisk walks, games and basic obedience, all of which will also build self-confidence in the dog. If that fails, gently distance yourself from your pet by completely ignoring all his ardent overtures until he finally gets the point or just gets tired and stops. That's a tough order since your natural instinct is to give extra love to your adopted dog. It may takes days or weeks to curb separation anxiety, but stand your ground. Reward signs of independence calmly, not excitedly, to avoid reviving clinging behavior.

When you're with your dog, don't absent-mindedly pet or fondle him. (He's got to earn this stuff, remember?) In many cases of separation anxiety, that constant attention from you only makes the stress worse when you're away and may even produce a more demanding animal when you're there.

This pooch watches for his owner to return home. Some dogs experience separation anxiety when separated from the people they love.

Your dog's favorite place to be is with you. Bring him with you on outings whenever you can.

Two recommended ways to cope with separation anxiety are desensitization and counterconditioning. Desensitizing (performing an action such as leaving home and returning in small time increments so often your dog stops being upset by your departure) may eliminate separation barking, but it may take weeks to transform daily comings and goings into a non-issue.

Set aside some time each day. Begin with actions associated with leaving: hold your car keys, put on your hat, your usual "going out" gestures. Do them several times a day but don't leave. Then leave and re-enter your house again and again. Remain out for varying intervals, at first very brief, then longer periods of time, staying within earshot to check if and when barking subsides. This may work better if you confine your dog away from the door in a crate or in a comfortable, disaster-proof area cordoncd off by a see-through barrier such as a baby gate or ex-pen. You can leave something that has your scent, an old tee shirt perhaps, for the dog to lie on. Leave a radio on while you're gone. Both music and talk-show stations are good substitutes for your voice. Return as calmly as you left and avoid eye contact to maintain the "cool" atmosphere. No big hugs when you release the dog.

Counterconditioning, which can be used along with desensitization, consists of teaching your dog to associate your departure with a pleasant experience. Dr. Nicholas Dodman, director of the Behavior Clinic at Tufts University School of Veterinary Medicine, says a timed-release treat such as a sterile marrow bone stuffed with peanut butter is an effective distraction. A favorite biscuit given as the dog is being confined and a second one as you leave the house can work well.

Dodman recommends you provide stimulating doggie activi-

rubber toy with peanut butter or cheese spread or drill holes in a Nylabone® and load it with the same goodies. You can also purchase these treats and supervise him the first couple of times you offer them. Also reduce his daily ration by the amount he eats through these offerings. You don't want to sacrifice boredom for obesity.

Dodman also suggest you provide "environmental enrichment" simply by giving your dog

Protect your furniture from chewing with a bitter tasting spray to make it undesirable. Unfortunately, in this case, it's too late.

ties or treats when you can't be home with him. "Many zoo animals have to 'work' for their food, which zoo keepers deliberately hide in cracks, crevices, trees and even Tupperware® containers," Dodman says. If your dog is a chow hound, try leaving a sustained-release food device—stuff a

access to a windowsill so he can survey his "territory." That's assuming the dog is trustworthy enough to be left loose or uncrated.

Disciplinary tactics will not eliminate or diminish separation anxiety. In fact it may harm your dog. Punishing a dog for something it can't control or has already done is pointless and cruel. The dog won't understand and will only become more stressed. When the dog displays symptoms of anxiety-driven behavior, give a "Sit-Stay" command, rewarding with treats and praise for the dog's compliance. Supplementing with such positive reinforcements can add to the success of your counter-conditioning program.

CHEWING

Chewing is probably the most common canine behavior problem and unfortunately it's very normal canine behavior. Dogs, especially puppies, chew for a dozen reasons, all of them deeply ingrained through centuries of chewing ancestors. So what's a human to do?

For starters, put your human things away where your dog or puppy can't get at them. No more dish towels on the door handle, slippers on the bedroom floor, open bathroom doors (think toilet paper), or open waste baskets. Your dog may actually tidy up your house a bit! Now give your

Give your dog his own chew toys, like a bright red Gumabone®, to satisfy his chewing needs.

dog his own chew objects, a few at a time. When you catch him chomping on your stuff, scold him with a firm "No," take it away and replace it with one of his own chewables, then praise him when he takes it. If he persistently returns to certain objects like your antique table legs, you can spray them with a bitter-tasting product to make them undesirable. Keep his toys in a container, preferably an indestructible one, where he can fetch them on his own. You may be picking up Nylabones® at bedtime, but it will prevent a lot of dental decoration.

BARKING

Barking is second only to chewing in the annoyance department. Most barking is stress-related. Your dog also needs to learn the "Quiet" command. If he barks excessively when you're present, hold his muzzle shut and tell him "Quiet," then praise him when he is, even if you're still clamped around his jaws. Repeat whenever necessary. If barking still persists, consult with your obedience trainer or a professional canine behaviorist.

JUMPING UP

Jumping is not only natural behavior for a canine, it's been reinforced almost from birth. When puppies stand on their tiptoes and peek over the top of their whelping box, they get picked up and are rewarded with a hug or kiss. They jump on the baby gates to visit us and we instantly scoop them up. By eight or nine weeks of age, their jumping has produced only positive results. Fortunately it's not irreversible.

If you hope to teach your dog not to jump on you or other people, you have to be consistent. As in your basic dog rules, you can't overlook it today, then expect it never to occur again.

Dogs literally jump for joy—when you come home, when visitors arrive, when they're excited about what's happening. To be successful, you must insist that your friends and family also never allow or encourage the behavior.

The best correction is teaching alternate behavior. Make the dog "Sit-Stay" when you come home or your friends come to the door. Insist he stay, then praise him calmly while he's sitting so that sitting is rewarded. If he jumps up, use the "Off" command and replace him in the "Sit" position. During the initial teaching phase, keep a short 6- or 8-inch line on his collar so you can yank him down with the "Off" command.

Avoid using traditional methods of correction—kneeing the chest or stepping on his toes—that can inadvertently harm your dog. For a persistent jumper, try the paw-hold when he jumps. Simply grasp his front paws and stand there, don't release them. Eventually he'll whine or try to pull away. Hang on a few more seconds, release and make him sit, then praise him because he sat. Easy to do, and it works!

That adorable pup who jumped up to greet you will grow into a seventy-pound Rottweiler. It is important to correct this behavior at an early age.

DIGGING

Dogs dig for many reasons, all of them logical to the dog. Breed heritage motivates many dogs to dig; it's in their genes. Some need an outlet for extra energy, dig out of loneliness or boredom, or just because it's fun.

Try to determine why your dog digs. If he digs to cool himself off in damp places, make sure he has adequate shade and water, provide him with a wading pool or house him in a cool area of the house. Is he digging to escape and why? For companionship, excitement if he's bored, to mate if he's still intact? Those are all fixable problems. Your fence should fit tight to the ground or even be buried a few inches underneath so he can't burrow under it.

If all else fails, try giving him his own digging spot. When he digs anywhere else, tell him "No" and take him to his spot, then praise him when he digs there. Obviously supervision is a must until his outdoor mischief is under control.

In dealing with digging or any other behavior problem, you should ask "Am I maintaining quality time with regular play, exercise and walks?" Dogs need attention and shared activities just like children do.

NIPPING AND BITING

Simply put, it's never allowed. Not even playful nipping and never a curled lip. If permitted or ignored, it will only escalate into more aggressive behavior. It's also easier and wiser to nip the nip-

Play biting should never be allowed, as it can escalate into more aggressive behavior. Discourage biting and nipping by grasping the pup's muzzle and growling at him.

ping in the bud when puppy is 7 pounds instead of 70.

Play-nipping can be discouraged by grasping the muzzle and growling "Errhhh." You can also turn your back or leave the room for 60 seconds, depriving puppy of your companionship. It works for some, sometimes. When a puppy growls, a scruff shake and a low-pitched, gravelly "Errhh" will send the Top Dog message.

If your adult dog growls, bites or curls his lips at you or other people, you should get professional advice. Discuss it with the shelter staff, your obedience instructor or consult an animal behaviorist. Never risk a dog bite.

Ginger

Ginger was adopted by Marianne Rogers and her family. "My children and I made two trips to the animal shelter before we found Ginger. I had wanted to find a beautiful dog like the Pyrenees I had in college. Ginger didn't quite fit the vision I had in mind. It wasn't love at first sight but it was within the hour. She had a red coat and such beautiful brown eyes.

Ginger was already a well-trained and healthy dog when we adopted her. She stays off furniture, doesn't beg at the table when we eat and isn't an unruly barker. She's a good watchdog and is very protective of "her" children. She's never lost patience with them, not even when mauled by a two-year-old. Ginger is happiest just being with the family and we're so happy to have her as an integral part of our lives. Every child (and adult) needs a pet to turn to for unconditional love, someone to turn to with their sorrows, fears and frustrations and joys."

"Ginger"

"Chub"

Chub

R oy and Pat Hummelshein got Chub, a terrier mix, on Halloween right after putting their 17-year-old dog to sleep. "We went to the shelter just to look but we instantly fell in love with Chub who was the WGEM Pet of the Week. He had been abused and his sign said, 'I just want someone to love me, not hit me.' He's been fine from day one and has never messed in the house. He uses his crate when we're not home but otherwise he's always with us, often sitting in our laps. He loves to play with his toys and run through the yard, yet he'll always stop as soon as you call him. He's been a definite joy and I'm sure the good Lord saved him for us."

Canine Amenities

CANINE GOOD CITIZENS

Every dog should be one. And now the American Kennel Club offers a certificate to prove it. In 1989 the AKC established an educational program to encourage dog owners to teach their dogs to be model citizens. Well-behaved

Toad, an Airedale-Shepherd mix adopted by Bernadette Postle, proved that shelter dogs can do it too. He and eight-year-old Becky Postle earned his Canine Good Citizen certificate with flying colors!

canine neighbors promote responsible dog ownership and are potent weapons against the anti-dog forces that threaten our rights as dog owners. Available to mixed-breed as well as purebred dogs, the CGC program awards certificates to dogs who pass a common-sense ten-step test.

1. Accepting a friendly stranger. The dog must not appear shy or resentful when the evaluator approaches and greets the owner.

2. Sit politely for petting. The dog must sit quietly while the evaluator approaches and pets him.

3. Appearance and grooming. The evaluator greets and speaks to the dog, handles it gently and checks it for health and hygiene.

4. Walking on a loose lead. The dog must walk easily at your side without tugging or resisting and without restraint from a tight lead.

5. Walking through a crowd. The dog must weave with you through a group of three or four people without evidence of shyness or aggression.

6. Sit and Down on command/ staying in place. The dog must obey these two commands, although you may give them more than once.

7. Come when called. You walk 10 feet from the dog, turn to face the dog and then call the dog. The dog may be left in the sit, down, or standing position. You may use body language or encouragement when calling the dog.

8. Reaction to another dog. You and your dog walk past another person and his dog and you shake hands with the person without your dog showing aggression or shyness. You may command your dog to stay.

9. Reaction to distractions. As you walk your dog, a tester drops a book, slams a door or performs another noisy activity. Your dog should not try to run away nor show extreme signs of fear or aggression.

10. Supervised separation. The dog is left alone on a leash with another person while you're out of sight. He should not bark, whine, howl or pace or register anything other than mild agitation or nervousness.

Most kennel and dog training clubs hold regular CGC tests for the dog-owning community at large. It's fun and your dog gets a diploma you can be proud of. That's an extra-special accomplishment for an adopted dog!

RESPONSIBLE OWNERSHIP: PRACTICE CANINE COURTESY

Dog ownership requires certain courtesies. Your dog is part of the community and you're responsible for how his presence affects your neighborhood. Your goal should be to make him welcome everywhere he might go.

Always clean up after your dog, whether in your own yard or in a public place. Plastic grocery bags make great poop scoopers to carry in your pocket.

Keep your dog on a leash in public areas. Even a dog who responds well to verbal control can "lose it" once in a while and tear off after a squirrel or a rabbit.

Teach your dog to accept friendly strangers, your neighbors and delivery people as explained in the CGC test. No one likes to be greeted by a noisy, snarling dog.

Make your dog a good example and keep him clean and well groomed. You need to be as proud of him as he is of you.

Take every precaution to ensure your dog doesn't damage your neighbor's property or garden. It will promote better friendship between you, greater respect for the dog, and better public relations within the community.

A well-behaved dog is the best deterrent to animal-rights legislation that could one day threaten your privilege to own a dog. Our dogs are too precious to risk.

Always clean up after your dog, whether in your own yard or in a public place. This Mini-Schnauzer keeps after his owner to make sure he does his duty.

Index

Other Books by the Author

The Proper Care of Golden Retrievers

One of America's most respected dog breeders and authors, Nona Kilgore Bauer has written a most comprehensive and readable guide on the care of the Golden Retriever, illustrated with over 200 full-color photographs of beautiful breed representatives at work and play. *The Proper Care of Golden Retrievers* covers all the basics of ownership, from selecting the right puppy, rearing and training, to keeping adults and seniors healthy and vibrant.

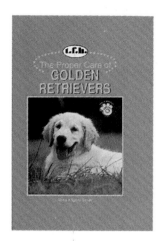

The World of the Golden Retriever: A Dog for All Seasons

The versatile and beautiful Golden Retriever comes alive on the pages of *The World of the Golden Retriever: A Dog for All Seasons* through the words of author Nona Kilgore Bauer and her team of guest-author professionals and in over 700 color photographs of Golden Retrievers from around the world. Rarely is a book truly worthy of the dog to whom it is dedicated—this volume is the exception. The most colorful and comprehensive work on the breed ever published, *The World of the Golden Retriever: A Dog for All Seasons* is the winner of the 1994 Dog Writers Association of America Best Breed Book.

Available from TFH Publications, Inc.